How To Books

Make Your
Mission Statement
Work

Make Your
Mission
Statement
Work

*How to identify and promote
the values of your organisation*

MARIANNE TALBOT

How To Books

Published by How To Books Ltd,
3 Newtec Place, Magdalen Road,
Oxford OX4 1RE, United Kingdom.
Tel: (01865) 793806. Fax: (01865) 248780.
email: info@howtobooks.co.uk
http://www.howtobooks.co.uk

First Edition 2000

British Library Cataloguing in Publication Data.
A catalogue record for this book is available from
the British Library.

Edited by Alison Wilson
Cover design by Shireen Nathoo Design
Cover image by PhotoDisc
Cover copy by Sallyann Sheridan

Produced for How To Books by Deer Park Productions
Typeset by Anneset, Weston-super-Mare, N Somerset
Printed and bound by Cromwell Press, Trowbride, Wiltshire

NOTE: The material contained in this book is set out in good
faith for general guidance and no liability can be accepted
for loss or expense incurred as a result of relying in particular
circumstances on statements made in the book. Laws and
regulations are complex and liable to change, and readers should
check the current position with the relevant authorities before
making personal arrangements.

Contents

Introduction

A mission statement is an explicit statement of the values of an organisation. It generates:

- the principles in accordance with which the organisation acts
- the standards against which it is willing to be judged.

As such a mission statement is a hostage to fortune.

If the organisation lives up to the values expressed in its mission statement, acts in accordance with the principles derived from it and meets the standards it generates the organisation will be securing its morale and strengthening its reputation.

If, on the other hand, it fails to live up to these values, it leaves itself open to charges of hypocrisy, weakness and/or ignorance from inside and outside the organisation: morale will be low and reputation shaky.

Successful organisations do not leave such matters to chance: they take steps to ensure that the values expressed in their mission permeate the everyday behaviour of everyone in their organisation. They ensure their mission statement is effective.

THE EFFECTIVE MISSION STATEMENT

The **effective** mission statement is one that is actively helping everyone in the organisation to live up to the values it expresses. It is a touchstone for every aspect of organisational behaviour. In expressing values that everyone in the organisation understands and shares it ensures that everyone in the organisation is:

- striving for the same goals
- working in accordance with the same principles
- adhering to the same standards
- fostering organisational morale
- securing the organisation's reputation
- determining the character of the organisation.

The six step process outlined in this book will help you to ensure that your mission statement is effective.

> Values must be based on actionable practices that everyone can recognise and emulate. They must be rooted in what actually goes on in a company day by day.
>
> Melvin R. Goodes, CEO, Warner Lambert

CLARIFYING ORGANISATIONAL PURPOSE

This book has been written for chief executives who are interested in:

* clarifying organisational purpose, the better to focus on organisational goals
* revitalising their organisation, improving morale and generating commitment
* managing change effectively and generating the support of everyone within the organisation.

If you are such a person (or hope to be) this book will help you to:

* make explicit the values that underpin organisational culture

* express these values in a 'living' mission statement

* implement systems by which to ensure these values permeate organisational behaviour.

Every organisation, whether in the public, private or voluntary sector, has **values**. These values underpin the 'feel', 'ethos' or 'culture' of the organisation. Quite often these values are not explicit. Nevertheless they are there and they are major determinants of morale, reputation and organisational character.

There are times in the life of every organisation when circumstances suggest a need to stand back and reflect on those values and to recognise the demands they make. Such circumstances arise, for example, when:

* a shake-up is needed to boost morale, secure reputation, improve performance
* radical change is imposed from without by developments in technology, innovations in the sector, new statutory regulations

- **change** is imposed from within by a new management, a crisis of **culture**, a merger with an organisation that does things differently
- a significant organisational failure mandates a radical re-think of organisational policy.

Such situations cry out for a return to first principles – to the values that underpin the organisational mission. If your organisation is facing any of these situations then this book will help you plan your response.

The six step process is designed to ensure that whatever has triggered your decision to stand back and reflect on your organisation's aims and values, your reflection will be practical, principled and productive.

> Discussion of our values proved to be a powerful bonding experience for everyone involved, creating the sense of community that had been lacking.
>
> Sir Richard Evans, CEO, British Aerospace

AIMING FOR THE LONG-TERM

Two assumptions underpin the recommendations in this book. They are:

- The more people who can be involved in making the decisions that affect them the better.
- The strong leadership necessary for success is consistent with a style of leadership that empowers others.

Involving everyone

> An Oxford college needed to raise students' rents. Last time it did this it notified students by letter just before the beginning of term. The students refused to pay and it took a term to calm things down. Next time the college thought about raising rents the Bursar asked to address the Junior Common Room. In his talk he explained why the extra money was needed and he outlined the alternatives to raising rents. He invited the students to consider other possibilities and to help make the choice. The JCR, having made a few suggestions of their own, voted almost unanimously to raise rents.

Research has shown that when people are involved in making decisions about changes that affect them, they will:

- be committed to, and prepared to take responsibility for, change
- be more innovative and creative in their response to difficulties, more willing to tackle inertia in themselves and others
- feel valued, trusted and empowered, more likely to identify with the organisation
- attach more significance to their work, understanding more about how it fits into the overall picture and its impact on others.

Such feelings and beliefs make a significant contribution to organisational morale.

> A state that dwarfs its men, in order that they be more docile instruments in its hands even for beneficial purposes will find that with small men no great thing can really be accomplished.
>
> John Stuart Mill, *On Liberty*, Chapter 5

Accordingly the first golden rule underpinning the recommendations in this book is:

Wherever possible and practical involve everyone affected by a decision in the making of that decision.

Adherence to this rule will admittedly make it more difficult for your organisations to make decisions. But it will greatly increase the effectiveness of those decisions.

> Giving people more autonomy or control over their lives does not lead to anarchy: it fosters accountability and responsibility . . . Power is not a fixed quantity, so if someone gains it, someone else must lose it. The reality is that everyone's power can be increased by effective participative decision-making.
>
> A. Leigh and M. Walters, *Effective Change*, p. 15

Leading by empowering

One of the key competencies for modern leaders is emotional intelligence. This involves:

- high levels of self-monitoring (awareness of one's own emotions)
- excellent listening skills
- the ability to:

- read social and emotional cues

- see things from others' perspectives

- adapt behaviour to suit the situation

- identify, express and manage feelings

- control impulses and delay gratification

- resist negative influences.

Emotionally intelligent leaders bring out the best in those they lead by empowering them, treating them with the dignity they deserve as partners in the quest for success.

> Leadership is not domination but the art of persuading people to work to a common goal.
>
> Daniel Goleman, *Emotional Intelligence, p.15*

Accordingly the second golden rule underpinning the recommendations in this book is:

Lead by empowering your people and by modelling the behaviour you expect from those who lead under you.

Adherence to this rule will create an atmosphere of confidence in which everyone feels free to share their ideas, offer constructive criticism and experiment with new ideas.

INTRODUCING THE SIX STEP PROCESS

The six steps are:

1. Identifying, with your community, the organisation's core values.
2. Reviewing current practice to identify:
   - present success in living up to these values
   - opportunities for further work.
3. Identifying concrete objectives for each department and individual.
4. Planning and implementing desirable changes.
5. Monitoring and evaluating progress and success.
6. Recognising and rewarding effort and achievement.

In taking **step one** you will be clarifying the purpose of your organisation in such a way that everyone understands its *raison d'être*. **Step**

two will help you to identify where your organisation currently stands in relation to the values identified at step one. This will enable you to build on your strengths and eliminate your weaknesses.

At **step three** you will involve everyone in deriving from the organisational mission practical objectives the achievement of which will help to secure your mission. At **step four** you will develop and implement strategies by which to ensure that these objectives are met. **Step five** involves setting up systems by which to ensure that your goals are being achieved by your strategies. **Step six** will keep everyone motivated in their pursuit of success.

FINDING YOUR WAY THROUGH THE BOOK

Chapters 1 and 2 take an in-depth look at the nature of values, comparing and contrasting the role they play in the lives of, respectively, individuals and organisations.

These chapters are a necessary preliminary. In reading them you will acquire the confidence you need to understand and discuss values with the others in your organisation and your community.

Chapters 3 to 8 will guide you through the six step process, exploring:

• the contribution made by each step
• practical approaches to each step
• illustrative case studies.

Chapter 9 considers ways to ensure that your mission statement remains effective over time.

1

Creating an Ethos

Ethos: the characteristic and animating essence of an organisation or community.

As a chief executive, one of your most important jobs is creating and maintaining a healthy ethos. An organisation with a healthy ethos is a vibrant organisation with a secure identity, one that all its staff understand and value, one that is successfully achieving its goals. If you succeed in building such an ethos your staff will be motivated, happy in their work and eager to put in that extra effort. This will greatly enhance your chances of achieving your mission.

The keys to a healthy ethos are:

- Encouraging staff and others to join you in identifying the values of the organisation.
- Encapsulating these values in a mission statement understood and accepted by everyone.
- Working with staff and the community to ensure that the organisation lives up to these values.

BUILDING THE FOUNDATION

Each of the keys to a healthy ethos depends on an understanding of shared values and the role they play in your organisation. But what are values? Why must they be shared? What have they to do with goals, principles and standards? How do they relate to morale and reputation?

To answer these questions it is necessary to understand the nature of values and their importance to us as human beings. In this chapter, therefore, we'll explore the connections between:

- values, principles and standards
- values, self-respect and our reputations.

In Chapter 2 we return to the role of shared values in organisations and to the mission statement that expresses these values.

Understanding values

Our values (noun) are the qualities that we value (verb). Here is the definition of 'values' on which this book is based:

> **Values are qualities that command respect and that generate:**
> - **principles to guide us in our thinking and our actions;**
> - **standards against which we judge ourselves and others.**

And here are some examples:

• happiness	• honesty
• love	• kindness
• health	• prudence
• truth	• self-discipline
• virtue	• courage
• freedom	• integrity
• beauty	• hope
• wisdom	• tenacity
• success	• temperance

There are values of different kinds. There are **moral** values (virtue), **aesthetic** values (beauty), **intellectual** values (wisdom) and **social** values (freedom). There are also values that seem closely related like love and kindness, truth and honesty. This is because this list includes both values *and* virtues. About the virtues, more below, for now we can think of them as values.

Commanding our respect

Values command our respect, they are worthy of esteem, we have reasons for valuing these qualities. They are not just qualities for which we have a personal preference. This difference is crucial.

Some of us like the colour red. Even so, we would not be surprised or concerned if a loved one disliked it. Nor would we try to persuade them otherwise.

But there would be something highly disconcerting about someone's claiming to *prefer* honesty or kindness. The implication that they wouldn't be surprised or concerned if someone else said they preferred *dis*honesty or *un*kindness, jars badly.

Most of us understand that human happiness and freedom, and so many of the other things that make life worth living, depend on the stability and success of the communities in which we live. And we see that the stability and success of these communities depends on people being honest, kind, trustworthy . . .

These qualities command respect because they are necessary conditions for the flourishing of human beings and the relationships and communities on which that flourishing depends.

To the extent that we believed someone who claimed they preferred dishonesty, we would think there was something wrong with them, we would be wary of them, we'd think they couldn't see why honesty is important. We'd certainly wonder why they were telling us this when it would be in their interests to keep quiet about it.

Honesty and kindness *matter* to us, in a way that (*eg*) colours don't; they *command respect*, they are not simply qualities for which we have personal preferences.

Generating principles

Values generate principles that guide us in our thoughts and our actions. It is not possible to think that a quality commands respect without thinking that we ought to possess it: to value honesty is to believe that one should be honest.

Because values generate principles they are essentially linked to behaviour. 'Should' beliefs are like rules, they guide us in our thoughts and in our actions.

Principles are general rules that apply in every situation. But it is often difficult to know:

- how a rule applies in a particular situation (would *that* action be dishonest/unkind?)
- what to do in cases of conflict (if telling the truth would hurt, should we lie?)
- how to resist the temptation to disregard such principles.

These difficulties ensure that our values make demands on us, that it is not always easy to live up to them.

Generating standards

Values also generate standards against which we measure ourselves and others. Insofar as we value honesty and believe that we should be honest, we will try to be honest, even when it's difficult. This doesn't mean we will *be* honest, of course, but it does mean that we will try.

And if we are honest (especially when it is difficult) we will deem ourselves successful; if not, we will believe we have failed. Honesty is a standard – an ideal – against which we measure ourselves.

This ensures that values are inextricably linked to our self-respect, another aspect of values that we'll discuss below.

We also judge others against the standards generated by our values. Insofar as we believe *we* should be honest, we also believe others should be honest. The principles and standards generated by our values are personal in that we make them our own, they are *not* personal in virtue of applying only to ourselves.

This property of the principles and standards generated by our values is called the **universalisability** of values.

VALUES AS GOALS

Values matter to us for one of two reasons:

- they are intrinsically valuable, good in themselves
- they are instrumentally valuable, good for the sake of qualities that are intrinsically valuable.

Intrinsic values

Human beings are unique: they can value things for their own sake rather than simply for the sake of survival and reproduction. We want our lives to have meaning and it is the qualities we believe to be intrinsically valuable – qualities like happiness, love, freedom, success, beauty – that give our lives meaning. On our deathbeds, we will decide whether our lives have been worth living by the extent to which we have acquired, and/or surrounded ourselves with, the qualities that are intrinsically valuable.

To see what you believe to be intrinsically valuable, try this:

> **Imagine that you are on your death bed, life ebbing away. Reflect on the things that have made your life worthwhile and the things you regret. What does this tell you about the things *you* value for their own sake?**

Someone once said that few of us would regret not having spent more time at the office, or not doing the housework. Yet in the midst of life these things are often given priority. Those who have had a brush with death often claim that it has helped them to sort out their priorities. This is because such experiences bring us face to face with the things we believe to be intrinsically valuable.

The qualities we believe to be intrinsically valuable are our life's **goals**.

Instrumental values

The qualities we value **instrumentally**, as means to the qualities we value intrinsically, are also goals, goals that we must achieve if we are to achieve our overall goals.

There are many layers of instrumental values. Every time we . . .
come to value some quality . . .
. . . for the sake of some other quality . . .
. . . we will come to value some further quality . . .
. . . for the sake of the second quality . . .
Values eventually shade off into personal preferences.

Values and virtues

The examples of values on page 16 include both values and virtues (the **right hand column** lists virtues). Virtues are those qualities possession of which enable us to live up to our values.

If we value truth, in other words, we *must* value honesty, because honesty (with ourselves and others) is a necessary condition of our discerning and preserving truth.

Our possession of the virtues, on this view, is so essential to our achievement of our life's goals that they have often been thought of as themselves intrinsically valuable.

We have seen that it is difficult, at one end of the scale, to distinguish our instrumental values from our personal preferences. At the other end of the scale, it is difficult to distinguish our instrumental values from our intrinsic values.

There is a philosophical tradition, going back to Aristotle, according to which there is only one intrinsically valuable quality: happiness. Other philosophers disagree, believing truth, wisdom, virtue, love, freedom and many other things to be intrinsically valuable. To look at what Aristotle meant by happiness, however, shows these views are not really so different.

To get a better understanding of *your* intrinsic values, try this:

Taking happiness – or any quality you believe to be intrinsically valuable – ask yourself exactly what you mean by it, and what you would have to do and/or be to achieve it.

A 'spider-chart' might help. Here is Aristotle's spider chart for happiness.

---

love (of and for spouse/partner, children, family,
friends, neighbours, God, humanity in general . . .)

dignity and virtue (self-respect and the respect of others)

security (reasonable wealth and comfort)

freedom to choose

joy

courage

HAPPINESS

beauty

fulfilment of personal potential

understanding

a sense of identity and belonging

peace

wisdom

growth

Some of the qualities associated with happiness might be considered *part* of happiness (and so intrinsically valuable), others *means to* happiness (and so instrumentally valuable).

Britain's second best paid company director Bob Edmiston pays himself well in order to give most of it to charity. His decision to set up the charity came after a dream in which at the gates of heaven God asked him what he did with his life and he answered "I made loads of money'. Then God then asked him what he did next and he answered 'I made loads more money'. He could, he says, 'see this conversation heading in a very bad direction'.

Getting values wrong

When it comes to personal preferences, anything goes. This is not the case with our values. Importantly, we can get our values wrong.

There are two ways of doing this:

1. We can value for its own sake something that it not valuable for its own sake (*eg* money).

* We can wrongly believe that achieving one thing will enable us to achieve another (*eg* that acquiring power will bring us love).

In the first case it is our intrinsic values we have wrong, in the second our instrumental values.

CONSTRAINING GOALS

Values are goals. They are also constraints on our pursuit of goals because of the principles and standards that they generate.

As we have seen, it is in the nature of general principles and standards that the way they apply in any particular situation depends on:

* which other rules apply in that situation
* how these different rules interact in that situation.

If you value both love and success, for example, and believe you should put energy into your marriage *and* your career, you face a conflict of values whenever you find you haven't enough energy for both. The value you place on love is a constraint on your pursuit of success, and vice versa.

Every such conflict requires us to make a decision, sometimes a very uncomfortable one. It is how we deal with such conflicts over a lifetime that determines whether or not we become the people we want to be.

DETERMINING CHARACTER

Conflicts of values cannot be avoided. And there are no general principles by which they can be resolved: each situation is unique. Sometimes love should come before success, at other times success should come before love. In each situation it is up to us to decide what is right.

We can take advice from others, of course, but even then *we* must decide whether to take that advice. Each of us is solely responsible for the way in which we live our lives.

The choices we make when values conflict:

* reflect our current character, who we *are*, because we are solely responsible for them
* form our future character, who we *become*, because their consequences determine the course of our lives.

Importantly no one decision (or even any small sub-set) accurately reflects our current character or predicts our future character. The person who values love over success will occasionally put success first, and even the most honest person may tell a lie when loyalty is at stake. Anyone who knew these people well would say that, on these occasions, they acted *out of character*.

It is a person's *consistently* putting love over success, loyalty over honesty, or vice versa, that gives us a grip on the sort of person they are. It also enables us to predict how their lives may go. It is the *pattern* of decisions that matters.

> The good of man is the active exercise of his soul's faculties in conformity with excellence or virtue. Moreover this activity must occupy a complete lifetime; for one swallow does not make a spring, nor does one fine day; and similarly one day, or a brief period of happiness does not make a man blessed and happy.
> Aristotle, *The Nichomachean Ethics*, book 1, 1098a 16–20

Values and habits

Habits are patterns of decision-making that reflect our values. Assuming that we have our values right in the first place, good habits accurately reflect our values, bad habits do not (although eventually they will as our characters change to match our habits). It takes effort on our part to form good habits, bad habits are far easier to fall into.

When we're busy, for example, it is easy to fall into the habit of consistently putting work before our relationships, even if we value our relationships at least as much as work. Soon our relationships will suffer. Conversely, important relationships can tempt us into consistently putting work last. Soon our careers will suffer.

If the habits we form are not true reflections of our values, they:

- can give the wrong messages about our current characters
- can prevent our becoming the people we want to be.

People who succeed in harmonising their values with each other are people with integrity. Such people are able successfully to resolve conflicts between their values in such a way that they truly live up to *all* their values.

Acquiring integrity demands a sustained effort and sound judgment on our part. It requires us to know ourselves and our values, to understand the demands that our values make of us, and to remain vigilant against developing bad habits.

> Integrity without knowledge is weak and useless. Knowledge without integrity is dangerous and dreadful.
>
> Samuel Johnson, *Rasselas*, ch. 41

It is here that we find the relation between values and self-respect.

GROUNDING SELF-RESPECT

If we form good habits and succeed, generally speaking, in living up to our values we develop increasing respect for ourselves. This will give us a robust core of confidence that will help to see us through the tribulations of life.

If we form bad habits and fail, generally speaking, to live up to our values, we will feel we're letting ourselves down. This will strip us of confidence. But the less confidence we have in our ability to live up to our values, the less likely we are to live up to them. A vicious circle can develop.

This, sadly, can turn us into **cynics**. There are two types of cynic:

- those who deny the real value of love, success, friendship *etc*,
- those who believe that values like this are really a reflection of power (you'll love me only if I have power over you).

Cynicism can turn us into bullies, people whose sole aims are to win power over others and avoid others winning power over them. It is difficult to imagine how someone cynical could be truly happy, or how they could be a positive influence in a community or organisation.

Low esteem can also prevent individuals finding happiness, though it is less destructive of others' happiness.

GROUNDING RESPECT FOR OTHERS

As we saw above, values are universalisable. Anyone who does not share our values, live in accordance with the principles they generate, or match the standards they set, will be found wanting.

This does not mean that *everyone* must *always* succeed in living up to these values: none of us can resist all temptation, avoid all error. And there are people whose values reflect the fact that their lives have been unhappy, violent and frightening. Such people have not had the opportunity to learn the right values. This is why, in judging others, we should always exercise compassion and understanding.

But it does mean that anyone who, on a regular basis, fails to measure up to the standards set by our values, forfeits our respect. We will view such people as untrustworthy:

- dishonest (saying one thing and doing another)
- ignorant (unaware of the importance of values)
- weak (aware of the importance of values but unable to resist temptation).

GROUNDING OUR REPUTATIONS

And just as we judge others against our values so we are judged *by* others. Our values and ability to satisfy the demands they make on us determine our reputations.

If we want to command the respect of others we must:

- subscribe to the right values (those that are truly valuable)
- live up to the standards they generate (at least most of the time).

If we succeed in doing this we will be earning a good reputation. This will invite trust and open doors that might otherwise be closed. A bad reputation will inhibit trust and close these doors.

The consequences of a bad reputation are very far-reaching. So far reaching, in fact, that everyone, no matter what their actual values, has an incentive to *claim* to share our values, principles and standards, and to *appear* to live up to them.

Even the most dishonest people have reason to claim to be honest, they even have reason to *be* honest most of the time. This is not only because most of the time it would be of no benefit to them to lie, but also because the best way to acquire a reputation for honesty is to tell the truth most of the time. Without a reputation for honesty it is difficult successfully to deceive anyone other than a complete stranger.

> No mask like open truth to cover lies.
> William Congreve, *The Double Dealer*, Act 5, scene 6.

If someone's actions do not accord with their words, it is always – and rightly – the actions we believe. If, embracing the right values, we find ourselves unable to live up to them, others will be unsure whether the discrepancy between what we do and what we say is the result of our having got into bad habits or because our values are not as they should be. We will be forfeiting their trust.

The values of individuals: a summary

Values are qualities that command our respect, they generate principles that guide us in our thoughts and our actions, and standards against which we measure ourselves and others. This means that values are:

* **goals** that matter to us, as valuable either in themselves or for the sake of something that is valuable in itself
* **constraints on our pursuit of goals** requiring us to make decisions about how life should be lived
* **determinants of our current and future characters** not only reflecting who we are, but determining who we become
* **inextricably linked to our self-respect** in virtue of setting standards against which we measure success (and failure)
* **inextricably linked to the respect of others** in virtue of underpinning our reputations.

In the next chapter we shall see that there are organisational equivalents for all these features.

Tim values health and friendship, believing he will achieve the former by regular exercise and a healthy diet, the latter by doing things with his friends. Tim's friends like going to the pub four or five times a week. Tim always eats and drinks too much at the pub, then he doesn't sleep well. The following day he is often too tired to exercise. Tim knows his lifestyle is undermining his health, he has started to feel he'll be letting himself down if he continues.

Tim resolves to suggest to his friends that they do something other than go to the pub. He vows that if they don't agree he will simply have to exercise will-power or find new friends.		Tim finds that his guilt goes away if he reminds himself of his intention to get healthy just as soon as he can. As soon, that is, as Don's wedding and Jim's promotion are out of the way.	
Tim's friends disagree. His resolve intact, Tim enquires about classes at the leisure centre. At first he feels lonely, then he starts to enjoy himself, to feel fitter and to make new friends. His self-esteem starts to rise.	Tim's friends don't agree. Tim goes to the pub anyway, where his mates tease him. Embarrassed, he agrees it is silly to worry about health. Years later someone suggests they do something other than go to the pub. Tim joins in the teasing.	Knowing that such events are frequent, Tim books himself into a health club for after the wedding. Ignoring his friends' teasing he continues to lobby them. Eventually one agrees to join him. Soon the others are also on side.	After the wedding Tim remembers he intended to get fit. Unfortunately, Tom is emigrating and his farewell is next month. Seeing no point in trying to get fit before that, Tim comforts himself with the intention of getting fit afterwards.

2

Understanding Organisational Values

Organisation: a structure of interconnecting parts with a purpose.

Armed with a secure understanding of what values are and of the role they play in the life of individuals, we can now examine the nature and function of organisational values.

In this chapter we shall compare and contrast organisational values with individual values, discovering significant similarities – and one important difference – between them. We shall conclude by considering the expression of organisational values in a mission statement.

In the next chapter we shall start our examination of the six step process.

MAKING THE LINKS

Given the differences between individuals and organisations, why should the importance of individual values convince us of the importance of organisational values? Why should we think, for example, that organisations *have* values, or that they have the same nature or play the same role as the values of individuals?

RECOGNISING THE SIMILARITIES

Individuals and organisations are more alike than we might think. For example, organisations, like individuals:

- make decisions

- act freely and responsibly

- have legal and moral rights and duties

- make and enforce their own rules

- are attributed beliefs, desires and intentions

- flourish and decline according to their own undertakings

- form habits, virtues and vices

- form relationships

- are praised and blamed

- attract loyalty, pride, affection, anger, resentment and hate.

These characteristics cause philosopher Roger Scruton to argue that organisations *are* individuals, complete with 'moral personalities'. And the law agrees with him. Organisations can be held legally to account in their own right (*ie* not in the person of any director or executive of the organisation) for such crimes as manslaughter, malpractice and negligence.

It has recently been suggested that a major car manufacturer used slave labour during the war. It is not being suggested that any of the current directors or employees of this company employed or condoned the use of slave labour. The suggestion is that *the organisation* is guilty of moral wrongdoing, that it is culpable and should pay compensation.

Not all organisations have all the features listed, nor do they have them in the same degree. And the law does not recognise every organisation as an individual. But to the degree that an organisation does have these features it has an identity – a 'personality' – of its own.

To what degree does your organisation possess these features? Does your organisation have an identity of its own? Could it? Should it?

Determining character

To the extent that we think of organisations as individuals, the values of an organisation should play a role precisely analogous to the role played by values in the life of an individual.

On this basis, an organisation's values will determine:

- organisational goals (both intrinsic and instrumental)

- the principles that guide organisational policies and strategies

- the standards against which the organisation should be judged.

And on this model, the extent to which an organisation lives up to the right values will:

- underpin its self-respect (its morale)
- underpin others' respect for it (its reputation)
- underpin its respect for others (*eg* employees, customers, shareholders, suppliers, its community).

The values of an organisation, it seems, together with its ability to live up to these values, determine the current and future character of the organisation: its identity as *that* organisation.

To get the values right, and to live up to them successfully, is to get the organisational culture and ethos right. And while such things are difficult to pin down, it is acknowledged by everyone that getting such things right makes a major contribution to organisational success. Just as individual happiness is dependent on an individual's living up to their values, so the success of an organisation depends on its living up to its values.

> No organisational strategy or programme can or will succeed without the appropriate organisational culture in place. Even the most expensive and elegantly designed building cannot stand without a sound infrastructure of beams and girders. Organisational culture is that underlying social architecture.
>
> R. Goffee and E. Jones, *The Character of a Corporation*, p. 8

RECOGNISING THE DIFFERENCES

So individuals and organisations are more similar than we might think. But clearly there are important differences, for example:

- organisations, unlike individuals, do not have subjective awareness
- organisations, unlike individuals, are *composed of* individuals and relationships between them.

The former mandates a small adjustment in our thinking about the role of organisational values. The latter has a major impact on the way values function in an organisation.

Striving for success

Human beings strive for happiness. They may differ in their awareness of this and in their beliefs about:

- what happiness is
- how to achieve happiness

but all strive to achieve it.

Yet it makes no sense to say that organisations strive for happiness because happiness involves a state of subjective awareness, something organisations lack.

The apparent disanalogy can be eliminated, however, if we think of individuals (including organisations) as striving for *success in achieving their goals*, particularly those goals – like happiness – that give life meaning.

The overall goals of organisations – intrinsic values – are those the achievement of which provides these organisations with their *raison d'être*.

Schools, for example, exist to produce wisdom, businesses to create wealth, hospitals and charities to promote security, health and well-being. This does not mean that all schools (for example) understand wisdom in the same way, only that all strive to produce it.

Every organisation has a purpose that defines it, thereby;

- making it an organisation of a certain kind
- providing its rationale
- determining its instrumental goals.

If an organisation is failing to achieve its overall purpose then the point of its existence can be called into question.

In thinking of organisations, therefore, it is the notion of success (in achieving its goals), rather than that of happiness, that encapsulates that which is intrinsically valuable.

To tease out what organisational success is to you, you might like to make a 'spider' chart for it.

High profits. . . .shareholder value   Sound reputation

    Community involvement   Excellent relationships throughout

ORGANISATIONAL SUCCESS

    Good morale   Customer loyalty

Good relationships with suppliers

    Excellent customer service

Your chart is likely to include things you believe to be an integral part of, and things you believe to be a means to, organisational success.

Understanding complexity

The second disanalogy between individuals and organisations is that organisations are composed of individuals, each with their own set of values and their own ability (or lack of it) to live up to them. An organisation, if it is large enough, might even be composed of individuals that are themselves organisations. And many organisations have within them departments that operate, or should operate, as if they were themselves individuals.

The complexity of organisational composition generates two types of value-conflict that have no parallel in the life of an individual. These are conflicts between the:

* differing values of constituent individuals (departments/organisations)
* values of the organisation itself and its constituent individuals.

The successful elimination or management of such conflicts is an integral part of organisational success. This ensures that the notion of *shared* values is of the utmost importance in the life of an organisation. Such a notion plays no part in the life of an individual. This is an extremely significant difference between individuals and organisations. It has a major impact on the role played by values in the life of an organisation.

Before we explore this impact let's re-visit the notion of a value-conflict.

Re-visiting conflict

It is in the nature of values to conflict (see pages 21–22). Each quality valued (intrinsically or instrumentally) generates a goal, and each is a constraint on the pursuit of the others. In order to live up to all their values over time, individuals must exercise sound judgment and sustained effort to negotiate conflicts wisely.

Organisational values are equally susceptible to such conflict. A hospital, valuing both compassion and efficiency, or a business valuing profitability, health and safety, will each find that such values inevitably conflict.

Organisations, like individuals, must exercise sound judgment and sustained effort to maintain integrity by balancing their values over time.

Let's now examine more closely the value-conflicts *peculiar* to organisations, those that underpin the importance of shared values.

Managing diversity
Every member of an organisation (let's say) values organisational success (intrinsically or instrumentally). But this does not mean they will agree on what success is or how to achieve it.

Some such disagreements energise, stimulate creativity, and trigger productive debate. Others are energy-sapping and creativity-stifling, leading to time-wasting squabbles, misunderstandings and irritation.

Consider, for example, the following two views of business:

1. **Our purpose is to create wealth.**
2. **Our purpose is to use profits to enrich the human soul and alleviate suffering.**

Differences of this kind (about which people can be quite moralistic) can undermine cohesion, making it difficult for people to work together. They arise, furthermore, in every sector. In education, for example, a debate rages about the extent to which schools should extend their remit from the academic to the personal and social aspects of life. In health the balance between prevention and cure has to be negotiated carefully.

It is easy, of course, to reconcile the two views above:

- Only wealth creation yields profits with which to 'enrich the human soul and alleviate suffering'.
- The best way to create wealth is effectively to market a product or service that 'enriches souls' and/or alleviates suffering.

But if the two views are operating implicitly the need for reconciliation can go unnoticed. And if different people are pulling in different directions this will inevitably undermine organisational integrity.

It is not only unrecognised disagreements about **what success is** that causes problems. Disagreements about **how to achieve success** also generate distress, especially when unrecognised.

Such distress can usually be eliminated through creative reconciliation if the disagreements that trigger it are brought into the open.

Minimising conflict
Conflicts between the values of organisations and their constituent individuals can also be a source of organisational ill-health. This can occur when:

- The values of organisations and individuals are incompatible.
- The organisation (and/or an individual) is failing to live up to its values.

A British organisation and an American organisation, each massively successful, merges. Each organisation has its traditional culture or 'way of doing things'. The British organisation prides itself on its speedy response to decision-making. The American organisation has prided itself on its participative democracy and the creative contribution made to decisions by everyone affected. In order to merge the two different cultures a massive values exercise, involving everyone in developing the vision, values and goals of the merged organisation, is undertaken. In bringing into the open the many differences in implicit and explicit beliefs about how things should be done, the new merged organisation harnessed the creativity of its employees and built on the strengths of each organisation.

Minimising incompatibility
Organisational cohesion is determined by the degree of compatibility between *its* values and those of the individuals who belong to it.

Most people understand this. Organisations, in recruiting, usually make some attempt to outline the values of the organisation and ensure that the values of prospective employees are compatible. Similarly, jobseekers usually apply to organisations whose values are roughly in line with their own.

Sir Ernest Shackleton, the famous explorer, recruited people for his expeditions by asking them whether they could sing 'or at least shout a bit with the boys'. Shackleton believed that a 'yes' answer to this question made it more likely the candidate would fit in with the others in the team than a 'no' answer.

But attempts to secure value-compatibility are not always successful. (Nor, depending on the market for jobs/labour, are they always made.) The result can be a clash of values that will benefit neither employee or employer.

Such clashes can occur without anyone embracing the wrong values, or failing to live up to their values. Their source lies often in differences of opinion about how to manage conflicts of value. One of the most common disagreements of this kind consists in an organisation's expecting to come first in the life of an individual when the individual puts family, community or social life first.

Susie is a sales representative. Her first job (in a small organisation where she stayed for five years) was fun, she had lots of responsibility and basked in praise when results were good (most of the time). She enjoyed close working relationships with colleagues, particularly enjoying Friday evening outings. When the time came for her second job she was delighted to hear that a nearby multi-national wanted salespeople. When her application was successful and she was sent on an expensive training course, she thought she was set. But, as a junior, Susie was given little responsibility, people were too busy to be friendly and good sales were expected not praised. Susie's sales slumped. Six months later she gave notice (marginally avoiding being sacked). The company were furious at having wasted money on her training. Susie was furious at the damage to her previously good reputation.

Walking the talk
Sometimes value conflicts occur not because of value-incompatibility but because an organisation or individual is failing to live up to their stated (or implied) values.

As we have seen (pages 15–21) we have *reasons* for having the values we (claim to) have, they are not just personal preferences. For this reason values command our respect and we universalise them, judging others as well as ourselves by their standards, holding everyone to the principles they generate.

Everyone, therefore, has reason to pay lip service to such values even if they have no intention of living up to them.

The frequency with which people and organisations fail to 'walk their talk' is often behind the cynicism about mission statements, after all no mission statement would ever read:

We intend to get everything we possibly can from our employees and customers whilst giving as little as possible in return.

Such a mission statement would not be praised for honesty, it would be condemned for stupidity. Yet sadly many people, if asked about the values that lie behind the actual practice of certain organisations, would express them thus.

Mismatches between what is said and what is done often go undiscovered in the first stages of a relationship. Those who don't uphold their stated values do everything they can to hide this (sometimes even from themselves) including offering plausible explanations for violations, or denying them entirely. And those who *do* uphold their values tend to assume that everyone is as trustworthy as themselves.

Violations of the principles and standards generated by our values

> The Hub Initiative, whose aim is to identify the values and aims of business and to help ensure that business lives up to these values and achieve these aims, has developed a means of measuring the 'gap' between what people believe the values of business *should* be, and what the values of business *are*. People are given a case study outlining a situation in which different values conflict. They are then asked two questions: (1) What do you believe the business *should* do in this situation? (2) What do you believe the business *would* do in this situation? Hub posed these questions to 2000 people. The results indicated a significant gap between people's perceptions of what the values of business *should* be, and what they perceive the values of business *are*. In particular a significant number of people believe that business puts profit before people.

rarely go unnoticed for long, however, because they nearly always cause damage. Once noticed the lack of trust engendered will itself threaten relationships.

> The organisation was pleased to have appointed Steve to customer services. He seemed just what they wanted. He would deal sensitively and speedily with queries and complaints, ensuring the customer was happy whilst tracking down the source of the problem and notifying those in a position to rectify it. They were shocked when, soon after his appointment, the partner of one of the directors, trying to change a faulty item, had been told – apparently quite rudely – that there was nothing wrong with the item. Although Steve denied this story, further enquiries made it increasingly difficult to believe him; others had been dealt with in the same way. And word was spreading fast as people didn't hesitate to tell their friends about the organisation's 'new policy'.

Individuals and organisations who do not walk their talk are not always doing wrong intentionally. They might simply be ignorant, unaware of the relationship between values, principles, standards and their self-respect and reputation. Or they might just be weak, always intending to do better, but never actually implementing the strategies needed to help them resist temptation.

Whatever the reason, though, for an organisation's (or an individual's) failing to walk their talk it will lead to disillusionment and relationship breakdown. The honest sales executive will not be happy if he is expected to lie about delivery dates to reach his sales targets. The compassionate doctor will not thrive if she is expected to reduce waiting lists by short-changing patients. Gifted teachers will wilt if appraised solely in terms of exam results.

Yet it is precisely these people who, by virtue of their values, are most likely to help their organisations achieve the goals these organisations represent themselves as having.

And it is not just the employer/employee relationship that can be undermined by value-incompatibility. Customers will get angry if an organisation fails to deliver on its promises, as will shareholders, suppliers and the community. Value clashes can haunt every kind of organisation.

The possibility of such clashes can be minimised by an organisation's taking active and self-conscious steps to avoid them.

CHANGING ORGANISATIONAL CULTURE

Value incompatibilities and clashes can and often do follow from a change in organisational character. Sometimes indeed an organisation will intentionally trigger such value clashes in order to bring about a change in organisational culture.

The appointment of a new chief executive or manager with a different style of leadership, for example, is highly likely to result in value incompatibilities and conflicts. For this very reason it is an excellent way of shaking up an organisation that is failing to live up to its mission, has low morale and/or a bad reputation.

For this reason too it is something to be managed very carefully if the organisation is *successfully* living up to its mission, has high morale and a good reputation.

Character changes will inevitably lead to a period of instability and discomfort for the organisation. For good or ill there will be resignations and early retirements as those who cannot live with the new values vote with their feet. Sometimes, if the established culture of the organisation is strong enough (or the backing of directors/governors sufficiently weak), it will be the new management that goes. There will almost certainly be dismissals.

This discomfort and instability will continue unless and until a new organisational identity emerges.

James has taught at a particular school for nine years. He has enjoyed his time there, his examination results have been excellent and he has always felt valued by pupils, colleagues and management. The new headteacher, determined to get the school even higher up the league tables, has told teachers to raise their examination performance by 10 per cent even if this means neglecting weaker pupils. James is starting to hate his work, believing that the school's claim to strive to fulfil the potential of every pupil (a claim he fully supports) is no longer true. He is not the only one who feels this way.

Organisational identity, however, as we have seen, is determined by organisational values. It depends on the existence of a set of core values to which everyone in the organisation, consciously or unconsciously, subscribes.

It is the organisation's core values, and/or its ability to live up to them, that must be changed (if what is needed is a change of culture) or that must be maintained (if what is needed is a continuation of culture).

Either way organisational success is determined to a great extent by the organisation's having a set of core values, and by the extent to which those values inform the behaviour of everyone in the organisation.

QUESTIONS AND ANSWERS

Value conflicts are ubiquitous: why should we believe that there are any shared values?
There is excellent evidence for the existence of shared values. In 1996 the National Forum for Values in Education and the Community, consisting of 150 people from across society, drafted a statement of the values on which they agreed. MORI showed this to 3,200 schools, 700 national organisations, did an omnibus poll of 1500 adults, and held focus groups of governors, headteachers and parents. 85–97% of respondents agreed with the values outlined and said they would be happy to see them taught in schools. Other sectors (health, business, the civil service) are also discovering such shared values.

If there are shared values why are there so many disagreements about values?
The existence of core values does not detract from the existence of unshared values. Also agreement on values does not ensure agreement on interpretation (what is truth?), ordering (I might put freedom before equality, you put equality before freedom), source (you believe it is God, I believe it is human nature), or application (you believe that respecting people means abortion is permissible, I believe it means abortion is impermissible). It is in reflecting on and discussing these disagreements that we discover how to live up to the values we share.

Why are disagreements about values so threatening?
Our values *matter* to us. Disagreements are evidence for error (on one side or both) and the behaviour to which such errors lead is nearly always damaging.

THE VALUES OF ORGANISATIONS: A SUMMARY

Organisations can be seen as individuals with 'moral personalities'. The organisational mission statement is a vivid expression of this personality in making explicit the organisation's beliefs about the:

- **Values** or goals that matter to the organisation, both as valuable in themselves and as a means of achieving that which is valuable in itself.
- **Principles** that inform the policies and strategies by which the organisation will achieve their goals.
- **Standards** against which the organisation will judge itself and is prepared to be judged by others.

Although both organisations and individuals value success, whatever that might mean to them, organisations are constituted of many different individuals. This complexity ensures that there will be many different views about:

- the nature of organisational success
- the means to organisational success.

Organisations can turn such differences to the organisation's advantage by:

- explicitly identifying its core values
- ensuring that its core values inform every aspect of its behaviour
- making use of these core values to ensure that individual differences stimulate energising and creative debate.

The six step process described over the next six chapters will help you to harness the creative energy of your people in the clarification of your organisation's values.

DISCUSSION POINTS

1. Some people think that in a pluralist society such as our own there cannot be shared values. What do you think?

2. Some successful organisations never discuss their core values. Do you think this means they don't have them?

3. Some people claim to be able to tell 'at a glance' whether or not someone is trustworthy. Do you think this is possible?

3

Step One: Consulting Your Community

Step one: identify, with your community, your organisation's values.

Step one involves consulting everyone on the organisation's values. It is your best opportunity to include everyone and lead by empowering. During step one you will be sending powerful messages about your good intentions and invoking the power of the community in your quest to achieve your mission.

The organisational mission statement that emerges from consultation will underpin the other steps of the process.

A FIVE MINUTE JOB FOR THE PUBLIC RELATIONS DEPARTMENT?

Your public relations department could write a mission statement in five minutes. This would cost you nothing. Their statement could well be indistinguishable from the result of consultation. So why consult?

You should consult because the benefits of consultation arise from the *process* of consultation, not its *product*. These benefits (listed on page 9) are highly desirable. They are worth repeating.

A successful consultation can ensure that everyone is:

- striving for the same goals

- working in accordance with the same principles

- adhering to the same standards

- fostering organisational morale

- securing the organisation's reputation

- determining the character of the organisation.

Asking your PR department to write the mission statement is a false economy.

QUESTIONS AND ANSWERS

What's the point of a mission statement? They all say the same thing.
When people discuss what really matters they largely agree. They certainly agree on the essentials. If this wasn't the case cooperation would be impossible. In consultation such agreement, and its importance to the smooth running of the organisation, becomes visible.

But surely it's all 'motherhood and apple pie'?
Some people believe that only *disagreement* is interesting. These people dismiss values as 'obvious'. But something's being obvious doesn't make it unimportant. Our values, however 'obvious', make serious demands on us. If they didn't it would be easy to live up to them. *Productive* disagreement is anyway parasitic on agreement. If we didn't agree on what we're talking about, its value and on what counts as evidence for truth, there'd be no point in disagreeing.

Surely it is not identifying values that is important but living them?
This is the rationale behind the six-step process. But we cannot reasonably be expected to live our values unless we know what these values are and what it is to live them.

SECURING RESOURCES

To consult successfully you need resources. You might have all the time, money, space, equipment, energy and expertise you need. Or you might not.

If such is your situation you might:

- identify your resources, then tailor your consultation to fit, or
- plan your consultation, then find the resources to match.

In the first case you'll know where you are. In the second you could achieve your ideal. This is a clash of values: security against excellence. Both are important. Only you can choose which, in your situation, is more important.

ENSURING STRONG LEADERSHIP

You might:

- be emotionally intelligent; an excellent listener and communicator

To find resources you might:
- Write a business plan. Include what you want to do, why, who will be responsible, the resources you need and why someone might help. With the plan approach business partners, banks, wealthy individuals connected with your organisation.
- Ask staff, governors, directors *etc* to help identify prospects.
- Consult a directory of charitable foundations to see if your project qualifies under their rules (be flexible and imaginative!)
- Contact local organisations and ask if they have rooms, equipment *etc* you might borrow.
- Learn about fund-raising by going on a course or reading appropriate books (see the Further Reading section).

- have a vision that enthuses others and secures their commitment
- have authority, both natural and derived from your position
- have the time, energy and enthusiasm to lead this project
- be a superb administrator, researcher and organiser.

If so you are the right person to lead your consultation. If not you need to identify someone who has these qualities. More plausibly, you need a team with these qualities.

None of these qualities is negotiable: strong leadership (and efficient administration) is a *sine qua non*.

PREPARING FOR CONSULTATION

Successful consultation requires serious preparation. You need to be clear about:

- who you will consult
- your short- and long-term aims
- how you will consult
- when (and where) you will consult.

DECIDING YOUR SCOPE

Each organisational 'constituency' sees your organisation from a different perspective. In consulting everyone you will see your organisation from a 360° perspective. Only this will give you a full picture.

Senior management assured us the values exercise was a waste of time. Morale, they said, was high, the organisation's reputation secure. Consultation revealed that their view was not shared throughout the organisation. Senior management were perceived to be getting all the perks and none of the pain. Middle and junior managers felt put upon and resentful, unrewarded for their hard work. And they were spreading word of this to potential recruits. Further investigation showed applications moving significantly downwards. Our – somewhat chastened – senior management are now wholly committed to our values project.

A senior personnel manager

'Everyone' includes your:

* immediate community
* extended community.

Identifying your immediate community

The 'immediate community' of a school includes:

* pupils

* teachers

* support staff

* management

* the headteacher

* governors.

In a business it includes:

* employees

* some consultants

* management

* executive and non-executive directors.

These boundaries are not rigid: schools might include parents, businesses regular customers.

Who would you include in your immediate community?

These are the people whose behaviour and states of mind determine organisational morale and reputation.

Identifying your extended community

A school's extended community includes:

- parents

- neighbours

- business partners

- local employers

- other schools

- voluntary agencies

- local faith groups

- the media

- local government

- emergency services.

These people are your 'critical friends'. 'Friends' in having your interests at heart. 'Critical' because your getting it right matters to them.

Who would you include in your extended community?

It is from these lists that you will decide who to consult at step one.

Including everyone

It is easy inadvertently to omit certain groups. It is often the most obvious groups who get left out. Schools, for example, have omitted pupils, businesses their secretarial staff. Such omissions can contradict the messages you are trying to give in consultation. You will want to check your list for such omissions.

Sometimes you might *want* to exclude a group. Part of the community, for example, might be hostile to your organisation. Only you can decide whether consultation would alleviate or exacerbate the situation.

Building a data-base

A data-base on which you record all names and contact details will be invaluable. You will use it in sending out invitations, questionnaires, reminders and feedback. As you proceed through your consultation important details can be added.

The Data Protection Act
No personal information about a living individual (including their address) should be traceable back to that individual. You will want to make sure that personal details are not included on returned questionnaires or that individual responses are not made publicly available.

IDENTIFYING YOUR AIMS

A successful consultation has a clear focus. Your aim is, of course, to identify the organisation's values. But this statement of aim hides a great deal of complexity.

The best way to clarify your focus is to identify your criteria of success. This involves formulating a clear statement of what you will count as evidence for the success of your consultation.

You might like to try completing, as concisely as possible, the statement.

My consultation will have been successful if by the end of it . . .

You will be clear about the aims of your consultation when you know exactly:

- What you want to learn from those you consult.
- What impact you want to have in consulting these people.

In considering your success criteria you will want to consider the following points:

Identifying ideals
Our values make demands on us. It is often difficult to live up to these demands. Value-conflicts, furthermore, ensure that it is impossible to live up to all of our values all the time. And in wanting to guard our self-respect and our reputations we often pay lip-service to values that don't actually guide our choices.

This means that if you ask simply: 'what are our values?' your question will be ambiguous. The two interpretations are:

- Which values *should* the organisation live up to?
- Which values *does* the organisation live up to?

Half your people will answer one question, the other half the other question. Clarity requires you to decide which question you are asking.

Laying the groundwork

You might decide to ask both. In asking the former you will be identifying your goals. In asking the latter you will be identifying your starting point. Your eventual aim is to move from your starting point to the achievement of your goals. At some point, therefore, you will *have* to identify both. Only then can you identify the gap (if any).

A leading company devised the following game by which to identify the gap between its espoused values and its lived values. Groups of 15 people, taken from a vertical slice of the organisation, were given a pile of magazines. They were asked to cut out and paste on flipcharts pictures representing the organisation's current culture and the culture they'd like to see. The final flipcharts provided the foundation for later meetings at which ways of bridging the gap were discussed.

In asking both questions you will be paving the way for step two, your review of current practice.

And it is not only step two for which, during consultation, you can lay the groundwork. You can also solicit ideas about:

- concrete examples of good and bad practice (steps two, three and four)

- improving organisational performance (steps three and four)

- barriers to improving performance (steps three and four)

- possible solutions to these barriers (steps three and four)

- what might count as evidence for success (step five)

- ways of monitoring improvements (step five)

- suitable ways to recognise and reward people (step six)

- beliefs about when recognition and reward are appropriate (step six).

Your consultation is a golden opportunity to harness the creativity of your people. But you will need to balance your desire to gather information against the loss of focus that could result from a multiplicity of questions.

You do not want to alienate your consultees by overworking them, confusing them or suggesting, by your behaviour, that you do not care about *them* but only about the information you can glean from them.

The impact of consultation

In identifying your aims it is important to consider the impact you want to have on consultees. Taking this into account does not make your consultation into a publicity stunt: it illustrates the importance you attach to your people, their well-being and their true opinions.

If in consulting you do not convince people that you are sincere in your desire to hear their true opinions, you will not collect the information you need. Acting on the misinformation you're likely to gather will not enhance organisational success.

The way you consult indicates the values that underlie your consultation. If you get it right even the most cynical might start to think they have it wrong. This will have a significant impact on people's responses to the initiatives that arise from consultation.

It is only sensible, in deciding your aims and identifying your success criteria, to give thought to the impact you want to have.

Once you have a crisp statement of your aims in consulting everyone, and of what will count as evidence of success, you are ready to plan your consultation.

GETTING YOUR TIMING RIGHT

It is essential, in consulting people, to:

- give people time to respond

- give yourself enough time to analyse responses

- avoid any busy periods

- make sure each stage of consultation follows in a coherent way.

The way to ensure you get the timing right is to construct a 'timeline'. This is a time-table showing all the different elements of consultation, their start-times, duration and expected end-times. Timelines are discussed in more detail in Chapter 4.

You might decide your timeline by working backwards from a good time to launch your new mission statement (an annual general meeting? the anniversary of the founding of the organisation?). Before you can decide your timelines, however, you will need to plan your consultation.

PLANNING YOUR CONSULTATION

There are six stages to writing a mission statement on the basis of a consultation:

1. preliminary research

2. the consultation proper

3. drafting the mission statement

4. a final check

5. finalising the mission statement

6. providing feedback to all consultees.

Let's look briefly at each.

Stage one: preliminary research

Your preliminary research will help you to:

- tailor your consultation to its audience(s) by enabling you to identify key

  - themes

  - interpretations

  - sensitivities

- test the way people interact

- identify likely disagreements

- ensure clarity of focus

- choose the best methodology for each stage

- check your timeline.

Your preliminary research will help you anticipate possible problems and decide appropriate solutions.

In the absence of such preparation fairly minor things (such as a
difference in interpretation or disagreements about your aim) can
take up an inordinate amount of time. Readiness with a response can
save time and instil confidence.

If yours is a small, close knit community, your preliminary research
might consist of a chat with key people. If your community is larger,
more widespread and/or complex, or if you are new to it, your preliminary research might include formal interviews, focus groups,
workshops and/or questionnaires.

During your preliminary research your subjects should:

- set the agenda

- define key terms
- talk at length
- offer opinions
- introduce sensitivities
- make suggestions.

Your job will be to:

- encourage subjects to talk freely
- listen carefully
- give positive feedback.

You might consider telephone interviews and/or video conferencing. Face to face contact, however, is more likely to elicit frank opinions, especially if your subjects have not met you (or each other) before.

The company newsletter, personnel files, the local paper or radio station will help you to identify suitable subjects for your preliminary research and start the conversation on the right foot.

You will want to involve people from across the communities you intend to consult. Don't forget to include the important sub-groups of each target group (*eg* pupils of different ages, salespeople as well as secretaries . . .).

In the light of information gathered during your preliminary research you might need to refine your criteria of a successful consultation.

Stage two: the consultation proper

You can consult people by:

- interview
- focus group
- workshop
- a consultative event
- telephone (one to one or conference calls)
- post
- email.

You might consult the members of your immediate community in one way (by interviews, focus groups and/or workshops?) and the members of your extended community in another way (by holding a meeting or sending questionnaires?).

Our rapidly growing publishing firm (employing 160 people) decided to find out whether our view of ourselves was matched by the view of our community. Our consultation had four components:

1. A telephone survey of the marketing media, agencies and competitors.
2. A visit to clients and people to whom we had unsuccessfully pitched.
3. Confidential one–one interviews with staff.
4. Half-day meetings of departments.

We started by asking general questions. We then narrowed down until we were asking for specific information on key issues. This exercise has given us a clear fix on our strengths and on our weaknesses. The results have formed the basis for our development plan.

In deciding your approach you will want to consider:

- practical matters (space, time, administrative support . . .)
- diplomatic matters (hostilities, sensitivities, pecking orders . . .)
- preferences (as identified during preliminary research)
- confidence and comfort (time to think, belief in procedures . . .)
- confidentiality (Chatham House Rules, The Date Protection Act).

One of the most effective ways of consulting people on organisational values is by getting them together and stimulating a discussion about values.

Such events can be large meetings of the whole community, or workshops with participants chosen to represent horizontal or vertical 'slices' of the organisation.

Such events can be held according to 'Chatham House Rules'. This means that although ideas discussed at the meeting can be taken outside the meeting, they cannot be attributed to any particular individual.

You will find plenty of ideas for holding consultative events on pages 53–55.

One infants' school involved everyone in identifying the school's aims and values. The meeting, in the school hall, was attended by parents, governors, local police and clergy, the caretaker, his wife, the cleaners, and staff from the junior school. The evening was run by two LEA advisers because the headteacher wanted to take part. After an introduction everyone was given a post-card size block of yellow 'post-its' and asked to write down five ideas (one per post-it) about what they wanted of the school. Everyone then chose one idea and wrote, on another post-it, how it might be achieved. Groups of 8–10 people were formed, each chaired by a teacher. Ideas were recorded on flip charts. Each group then had two minutes to present their ideas. The advisers then asked for four volunteers to help the school condense the results into a draft statement of aims and values. When written this was circulated for comment. The final statement, revised in the light of comments, was presented to a formal parents' meeting and unanimously agreed. Parents are delighted with the process. They say they feel their views are really being listened to. The head, initially nervous, was very pleased with the outcome. The school is adopting a four-year cycle so every parent has an input into the school's aims and values.

Stage three: the drafting of the mission statement
The outcome of the consultation proper will be a lot of:

- information about the organisation, its values and its living of these values
- goodwill and energy.

Your task is now to build on the latter by using the former to draft your new mission statement and provide feedback to participants.

To draft your new mission statement you need to analyse all your information. This involves:

- identifying key themes and ideas

- identifying different formulations of the same themes and ideas

- noting favoured words and phrases

- mapping relationships between themes and ideas

- identifying th consensus on overall organisational purpose

- identifying beliefs about means by which to achieve this purpose.

Having done this you will need to try to capture these beliefs about means and ends as concisely as possible in a vocabulary that will resonate with consultees.

Your draft should have the following qualities:

1. It is clear, concise and will be understood by all.
2. It is flexible enough not to need re-writing in two years' time.
3. It accurately captures the *raison d'être* of your organisation.
4. It outlines your intrinsic and your instrumental values.

You might also find it useful to include definitions of key words.

Our mission is to be the best and most successful company in the airline business. We shall do this by:
  Making safety and security a priority
  Delivering strong and consistent financial performance
  Securing a leading share of air travel business worldwide with a significant presence in all major geographical markets
  Providing overall superior service and good value for money in every market segment in which we compete
  Excelling in anticipating and quickly responding to customer needs and competitors' activities
  Sustaining a work environment that attracts, retains and develops committed employees who share in the success of the company
  Being a good neighbour, concerned for the community and the environment.

British Airways mission statement

Stage four: conducting a final check

In conducting a final check you can make sure that your draft mission statement:

- uses the language that consultees accept and understand

- accurately expresses the vision that emerged in consultation

- expresses the ideals expressed by consultees

- includes specific ideas constantly expressed by consultees

- does not reflect personal bias.

Your final check might consist of:

- further interviews and/or focus groups

- a postal survey.

You might choose to check the draft with all consultees, or simply with a representative group. This final check will give you (and others) the confidence of knowing that your final mission statement will encapsulate the vision expressed in consultation.

You might decide at this point to check your draft with an organisation such as the Plain English Society. They will help you to avoid formulations that sound pretentious and/or ambiguities that might mislead.

It should be made clear to those consulted at this point that this is not a re-run of the consultation proper, but simply a means of checking that the spirit of the consultation has been captured. Do not be tempted to re-write completely unless you are convinced by participants that you really have got it wrong.

Stage five: finalising the mission statement

Once you have made your final check you are ready to finalise your draft. At this point you should simply be dotting 'i's' and crossing 't's'. If you do need to re-write then return to stage three, get out all the documentation from the consultation and start again. it might be better should this be necessary to hand on the job to someone who can start afresh. It is important that this person was at the consultation. Only then are they likely to be able to capture the spirit of that consultation.

Once you have refined your draft you are ready to launch your mission statement and embark on the next steps of the process.

Stage six: providing feedback

It is important at some point to provide feedback to everyone who was involved at any stage of your consultation. This is the ideal point at which to provide that feedback because you can share with them the fruits of their labour: the final mission statement.

You might also like to explain to them the steps you intend to take to achieve this mission. This will involve outlining the next five steps of the process. These steps are discussed in Chapters 4 to 8.

Before we turn to them, however, let us look at some practical tips for conducting:

- interviews
- focus groups
- consultative events
- questionnaires.

Conducting interviews

The successful interviewer:

- explains what the interview is for and why their subject was chosen
- offers a choice of days and times
- arranges a room that:
  - affords privacy
  - is comfortable
  - is sensitively arranged (*eg* no intruding desk)
- provides refreshments
- starts by saying:
  - they appreciate their subject's coming
  - why their subject was chosen (again)
  - what the purpose of the interview is (again)
  - confidentiality will be respected
- secures permission to record (note-taking interferes with listening)
- actively listens, provides positive feedback, probes for further information
- concludes by:
  - thanking their subject
  - telling them what will happen next
- transcribes their recording as soon as possible.

Conducting focus groups

The ideal focus group:

- has 8–12 members (so everyone contributes and no-one dominates)
- is constituted of:
  - different representatives from one group, or
  - representatives from different groups
- might be one of a number of such groups
- is not constituted of volunteers (who won't be representative)
- is held in a large, sensitively arranged, comfortable room
- does not last more than 75 minutes without a break
- is such that members know:
  - why they are there
  - who everyone is
  - that they are being recorded
  - that confidentiality will be respected
  - what time they'll finish
- concludes with a resume of next steps and a thank you.

Again you will want to transcribe your notes or tapes as soon as possible.

Holding consultative events

It is rarely *necessary* to hold a special event for your consultation. Here are some examples of pre-existing opportunities:

- departmental away-a-days
- training days
- planning meetings
- board meetings
- management meetings
- open days
- parents' meetings
- residential conferences
- summer fetes
- shareholders' meetings
- the annual general meeting
- product launches.

You will need to take care that your participants will have the energy (and you the time) to enable you to achieve your aims.

Specially organised events, on the other hand, can underline the organisation's commitment to this process.

Such events could be:

- morning, afternoon or evening meetings
- whole day conferences
- teatime to teatime conferences
- two day midweek or weekend conferences.

They can be held:

- in the organisation's own buildings
- in meeting rooms borrowed from a partner
- at a hotel (local or otherwise)

- at a conference centre
- at a football stadium or racecourse
- in the gardens or grounds.

Such events might launch the consultation, mark its culmination, or *be* the consultation.

People's thoughts must be accurately noted. You might consider recording the proceedings (perhaps on video?). Or you might appoint 'scribes' to make a written record.

Your event(s) are more likely to be successful if:

- **attendance is voluntary but pre-event publicity is compelling** (invite a celebrity, run a draw, put on a play/video, involve the local media . . .)
- **attendance, though non-voluntary, is rewarded** (suspend normal work, invite partners/families, go orienteering, choose a luxurious hotel, provide opportunities to try go-carting, ballroom dancing, skiing . . .)
- **you start with an attention-grabbing talk or activity** (invite an inspirational speaker, use special effects, make participants cry or laugh, emotionally move them . . .)
- **everybody can make an active contribution** (break into groups, get participants moving, get people sticking things on boards, standing on chairs . . .)
- **activities are short, varied and fun** (ask for stories to illustrate good or bad practice, ask people to cover the walls with post-its on which values are written . . .)
- **people can socialise, eat and drink** (plan time for mingling, approach local catering companies or department stores for refreshments, serve beer or wine if appropriate . . .)
- **accommodation is spacious and comfortable** (ensure the temperature is right, chairs are comfortable, people can see and hear properly . . .)
- **you have all the equipment you need** (overhead, video or slide projectors, microphones (in working order), water and short biographies for speakers, flipcharts, supplies of pens, post-it notes, paper, blu-tack, sellotape . . .)

Such consultative events can be great fun. Managed well they enhance relationships throughout the organisation and generate a great deal of goodwill.

As part of our attempt to identify people's priorities we placed ten flip charts around a large room. On each we wrote a value and a related project. A cost was attached to each. We gave everyone £10,000 of monopoly money and asked them to 'spend' their money as they chose. At the end of the game our priorities were clear. Everyone complained that they would have liked more money – but we already knew we couldn't do justice to *all* their projects. Now we know exactly which ones have popular support.

Using questionnaires

Questionnaires can be used as the basis for a telephone survey, a postal survey, or indeed a consultative event.

A successful questionnaire:

- is used for named people who are:
  - expecting it
  - have reason to complete it
- is tailored to respondents' interests and sensitivities
- arrives at a convenient moment
- is brief, clearly focused, easy to complete
- has clear instructions, numbered questions and pages
- has a clear return date and address
- asks unambiguous questions that will elicit useful answers
- is accompanied by a pre-paid reply envelope (if possible)
- is colour-coded by type of respondent (if part of a set)
- is such that responses are easy to analyse
- is returned at a convenient time for analysts.

You might send a different questionnaire to each group, although you will probably want a set of core questions to appear on each.

Some of your questions should be 'closed' so that you can collect some quantitative data (ten per cent of respondents agreed . . .).

There are different types of 'closed' question as follows:

1. Yes/no or closed multiple choice
   Gender:
   ❏   Male
   ❏   Female

2. More than one choice
   Which values do you deem most important?
   (tick appropriate boxes)
   ❏   trust
   ❏   honesty
   ❏   kindness

3. Graded responses
   'Profit comes before principle.' Do you:
   ❏   Strongly agree
   ❏   Agree
   ❏   Disagree
   ❏   Strongly disagree

4. Ordered choice
   Please order the following using a scale from 1–5 (1 = highest)
   ❏   Integrity
   ❏   Wealth
   ❏   Kindness

Closed questions should have a minimum of two choices. If, for example, you ask the following question:

Please tick the box if you use a code of practice   ❏

You will not know whether those who don't tick the box *don't* use a code of practice, or simply haven't answered the question.

Questions should be written so that all respondents are capable of using one of the responses. Ambiguity should be avoided and you should be careful of confusing issues, as this question illustrates:

Please indicate how you use the code of practice in your job:
   ❏   Consulting the code of practice is an integral part of my job
   ❏   I occasionally consult the code of practice
   ❏   The code of practice is not helpful

The last question looks for a response not on the use of the code of practice but on its usefulness.

Not all the questions should be closed or respondents will not feel they can express their opinions. 'Open' questions give people a chance to express themselves. They can also elicit new ideas. Examples of open questions include:

- What do you think of ....
- How would you respond to ....
- What is your opinion of ....

Be careful to leave enough room for a full reply. A closed question can be 'opened up' by a space for comments.

Once you have written your questionnaire it would be sensible to hold a dummy run. This will help you to eliminate obvious 'howlers' and to avoid asking unanswerable or ambiguous questions or questions that elicit unwanted or hostile responses. You can conduct a dummy run on the people involved in your preliminary research or on partners, children and/or friends.

SUMMARY

Step one involves consulting your community on the aims and values of the organisation. In preparing for consultation you need to decide:

* who to consult
* your short- and long-term aims
* how you will consult
* when (and where) you will consult.

In planning how to consult there are six stages to consider:

1. preliminary research
2. the consultation proper
3. drafting the mission statement
4. a final check
5. finalising the mission statement
6. providing feedback to consultees.

In planning each stage you might draw on any combination of the following:

* interviews
* focus groups
* workshops
* consultative events
* telephone surveys (one to one or conference calls)
* postal surveys
* email surveys.

The outcome of step one will be a brand new mission statement, one that encapsulates the core values of the organisation.

QUESTIONS AND ANSWERS

What if everyone disagrees with each other?
This is most unlikely. There might be disagreements about means versus ends, different interpretations of values or about the ordering or application of values, but not about the key aims and values themselves.

How should I deal with the sceptics?
By having your arguments ready. Try listing three reasons for thinking (a) that there are common values (b) that consultation on the organisation's core values will enhance organisational success.

4

Step Two: Reviewing Current Practice

At step one, in consultation with your community, you wrote your mission statement. Step two involves conducting a review of current practice. This will show you the extent to which you are already:

- achieving the aims and
- living up to the values

expressed in your mission.

In conducting your review you will identify organisational strengths and weaknesses in relation to the achievement of your mission. This will enable you to build on the former and eliminate the latter.

INVOLVING EVERYONE

Everyone, at every organisational level, should be involved at step two. All can benefit from reflecting on their:

- job, the way it's done and its place in the scheme of things
- department, its function and relations to other departments
- teams, their contribution and the way they function.

Such reflection will increase clarity about:

- What they do.
- Why they do it.
- How doing it contributes to organisational success.
- The extent to which their success depends on others.

Such clarity reveals the structure of the organisation: the way each part fits with every other part. Clarity about organisational structure will help you.

- understand relationships throughout the organisation
- maintain the coherence of the organisation
- avoid unnecessary duplication of effort
- track the causes and effects of good and bad practice.

REVIEWING EVERY ASPECT OF ORGANISATIONAL BEHAVIOUR

Your review needs to be comprehensive. No part of the organisation should escape scrutiny. You will want to examine:

- departments
- committees
- teams
- individuals
- relationships, formal and informal
- power balances
- communication systems, internal and external
- written policies, strategies, procedures and rules
- resources and their allocation
- the environment, internal and external
- the use of time.

This list is not exhaustive, you may well be able to add to (or subtract from) it on the basis of your knowledge of your own organisation and its structure.

> In a survey of 5,500 adults two thirds of those surveyed claimed that they regularly worked longer than their basic working hours. More than 60 per cent said the speed of work, effort put into the job and working hours had increased over the last five years. The same number claimed to have been demotivated by these changes. Forty-four per cent claimed that management could not be trusted to look after their best interests.

Deciding your timetable

You will need to decide in advance when you will have completed your review. Care needs to be taken in deciding how much time to devote to it. Too little time and you might fail to gather enough information. Too much time and the information you gather might be out of date before you can analyse it.

CONDUCTING YOUR REVIEW

Your review will involve gathering information about:

- The contributions made to the organisation's achievement of its overall mission.
- The contributions made to the achievement of each of the organ-

isation's instrumental goals.
- The way in which these contributions are made.
- The relationships that support these contributions.
- The key values that inform these contributions and the way they're made.
- The morale and reputation, or the impact on organisational morale and reputation, of each aspect of the organisation.

If one of the statements of your expanded mission statement is 'enable our employees to give of their best' you might examine every aspect of organisational behaviour in the light of questions such as:

- Does this (department, system, procedure) encourage and enable our employees to give of their best?

- How does this (department, system, procedure) enable our employees to give of their best?

- Is there anything about this (department, system, procedure) that prevents or makes it difficult for employees to give of their best?

- Do the employees who come into contact with this (department, system, procedure) believe it enables them to give of their best?

- Could this (department, system, procedure) be improved to encourage and/or enable employees to give better?

In each case you will want to:

- **analyse** current practice so you know *what* you are doing, and
- **evaluate** current practice so you know *how* you are doing.

It is only by doing both that you will be able to identify all your strengths and your weaknesses: the *actual* and *potential* contributions made to organisational success by each aspect of the organisation.

GATHERING EVIDENCE

In acquiring the information you need you will find it necessary to:

- gather 'hard' facts such as:
  - staff turnover
  - absenteeism
  - bullying, abuse, harassment
  - complaints

- awards won
- sales figures
- league table placements
- mortality figures
- donations received
- participation rates
- rates and speed of response to enquiries, applications *etc*

• solicit opinions from people across the organisation about:
  - morale
  - reputation
  - relationships
  - the use of space, time, resources
  - the distribution of power
  - what works well
  - what works badly
  - barriers to success
  - the improvements that might be made

• consider different interpretations of both.

It is particularly important not to neglect consideration of different interpretations of the facts and opinions you gather.

If, for example, you discover that last year there were *no* incidents of bullying, this might be because:

• Relationships are excellent, people are behaving well and there is no problem with bullying.
• You do not have any systematic means of recording incidents of bullying.
• Bullying is so bad that no one dares report incidents despite the excellent system.
• The system for recording incidents of bullying is so inefficient that people prefer to deal with it themselves.
• Organisational culture is such that people do not recognise incidents of bullying as such.
• The reward system is such that there are disincentives for recording bullying.

It is only by considering each of these facts and opinions in the light of all the others that you will begin to form a true picture about organisational practice.

It is particularly important to recognise that much organisational practice is implicit. Many rules, for example, are not written down, they are simply part of 'the way things are done round here'. It is often in these unexpressed rules, regulations, procedures and processes that the true values of the organisation are made manifest.

The very fact that these 'rules' are implicit, exhibited only in what people do, can make them difficult to identify. These difficulties must be overcome if you want to formulate a true picture of where your organisation currently stands with respect to its values. Several methods for making explicit the implicit 'rules' of your organisation will be discussed below.

CHOOSING YOUR METHODS

You can make a useful start by gathering as much documentary evidence as you can. Useful documents might include:

* job descriptions
* codes of conduct
* statistics
* annual reports
* representations of organisational and departmental structure
* written policies, rules, systems
* proformas/standard letters/questionnaires
* schemes of work
* staff handbooks/training manuals
* prospectuses/handouts/fliers and other promotional materials.

It is not just the content of these documents you need to consider. You will find it useful to reflect on whether such documents are:

* interesting and easy to understand
* clear and concise
* informative and accurate
* appropriate (not patronising, hectoring, insulting or impersonal)
* widely (and appropriately) distributed
* actually distributed to the appropriate audience.

An analysis of written material may provide you with some questions to ask as you conduct your review.

> John had looked forward to his first day at his new company. But on his way home he was feeling depressed and insecure. The organisation appeared to have no system by which to help new employees find their way around. He had been given a staff handbook, but this was so long it was daunting and certainly not something he could sit down and read at one session. It seemed to be so full of rules he was afraid to act for fear of breaking one. The person who greeted him had shown him a desk and asked him to check some spreadsheets, but without giving him any indication of why he was doing it, when he needed to do it by or to whom he should give it when finished. People were friendly but so busy that he hadn't liked to ask for help. John was not looking forward to his second day.

In gathering opinions you will need to be creative in order to ensure that the picture you construct is accurate.

There are many factors that might prevent you acquiring an accurate picture of employees' opinions. These include employees':

- ignorance
- wanting to please
- desire to cover themselves
- desire to protect others
- loyalty to friends, bosses and departments
- suspicion about your motives in asking
- misunderstanding of what you want to discover
- belief their benefits might be affected.

This is by no means an exhaustive list. If you want to construct an accurate picture of organisational practice you will need to take steps to eliminate or allow for these factors. Furthermore you need to do it consistently with the values expressed in your mission statement. This will probably mean that your methods need to be as transparent as possible. They will need to respect people's loyalty, desire to protect themselves and others and defuse their suspicions about motives and possible harm to themselves and others.

Gathering evidence
Here are some possible approaches to the gathering of evidence:

1. **'Sensing'** – use focus groups to 'sense' organisational morale, reputation and stakeholder attitudes about particular aspects of organisational behaviour or provision.
2. **Shadowing** – shadow an employee/pupil/patient/fund-raiser for a day (or a week) to see how the organisation looks from their perspective.
3. **Mystery 'customers'** – employ 'mystery' shoppers, parents, patients, carers to report on their treatment (make sure employees know about such shoppers).
4. **Questionnaires** – the old stand-by, but no less useful for that. Try to provide feedback to avoid cynicism and try not to stretch people's goodwill by sending them out too often.
5. **Walkabouts** – walk around departments and outlets talking to employees and asking them about themselves, their work and the organisation. Take lunch in the canteen. Watch people arrive and depart. Sit in on training sessions, departmental awaydays.
6. **Benchmarking** – visit other organisations, both in your sector and sectors quite different from your own. How do they do things? Is morale high? What makes you say that? Is there anything you might learn?
7. **Interviews** – conduct or ask outside consultants to conduct interviews with stakeholders.
8. **SWOT analyses** – invite all stakeholders to conduct analyses of strengths, weaknesses, opportunities and threats.
9. **Critical Incident analyses** – using illustrative case studies ask people to say how certain imaginary situations would be dealt with by the organisation. Is this how they believe these situations *should* be dealt with?
10. **Helpful friends** – ask what advice people would give to a friend or relative about to start work with the organisation?

These methods are not, of course, mutually exclusive. You could combine several of these methods, checking their results against each other.

TROUBLESHOOTING

To embark on step two is to show that the identification of the organisation's values was not just an exercise in public relations. The realisation that things really are going to change is likely to trigger some resistance to your activities.

You might usefully treat such resistance as an opportunity to rehearse the arguments for what you are doing. Certainly you should ask people to share with you their reservations. Some of them may reveal real difficulties in your approach. The fact you have listened can only add to your credibility.

Other reservations you may find quite difficult to grasp: resistance to change is often emotional rather than rational. Your task will be to demonstrate that the perceived negative consequences of change are outweighed by the positive consequences. You can only do that if you know what the negative consequences are perceived to be. You will need to tease out people's fears and address them head on.

Be aware that people can resist change actively or passively. Active resistance can involve generating and maintaining the sort of whispering campaign that undermines confidence. Passive resistance can involve simply failing to provide information or do what is asked: something always getting in the way.

Again you can only be open and honest about what you are doing, and about what you perceive as their resistance. This might encourage those who are resisting to be as open and honest about the fears that are causing them to act as they do.

In the final analysis there may be people you cannot carry with you. Only you can decide whether their continued presence in the organisation will inhibit organisational success.

CONCLUDING THE REVIEW

The information gathered from each area of the organisation will need to be collected and collated. Then it will need to be assimilated, summarised and expressed in a clear picture of current organisational practice. It is at this point that organisational strengths and weaknesses will become clear.

Departmental, individual, systematic weaknesses will, of course, become clear before this point.

Step three will provide an opportunity to set objectives by which to build on these strengths and eliminate these weaknesses.

SUMMARY

At step two you will conduct a review of every aspect of organisational practice by methods devised to give you a complete and accurate picture of your organisation.

This will involve gathering:

• hard facts, and
• opinions

and considering different interpretations of these facts and opinions. This will enable you to:

- analyse, and
- evaluate

current practice in the light of your organisational mission. You will be rewarded by an accurate and full picture of:

- organisational strengths (which can then be celebrated)
- organisational weaknesses (which can then be addressed).

In Chapter five we shall be considering how to set objectives by which to build on these strengths and eliminate these weaknesses.

5

Step Three: Identifying Concrete Objectives

Concrete objective: a specific and clearly defined goal.

Step three involves the setting of concrete objectives by which to build on the strengths and eliminate the weaknesses identified at step two.

In setting concrete objectives, and encouraging others to do so, you will:

- Clarify organisational, departmental and individual focus.
- Close the gap between the values you espouse and those you live.
- Reinforce key messages about the organisational mission.
- Generate a practical understanding of organisational aims and values.

The last is particularly important: in setting concrete objectives the fine sentiments expressed in the mission statement start to acquire practical meaning. Only this will ensure they engage with everyday behaviour.

When this happens the vision expressed in your mission statement starts to become a reality.

INVOLVING EVERYONE

Everyone needs to be involved in the setting of objectives. This is because objectives need to be set for every individual, as well as every department and for the organisation itself.

In each case the objectives set need to reflect objectives elsewhere. Every objective set should reflect the related objectives for:

- individuals

- teams

- departments

- the organisation.

And they need to be informed by the review of current individual, departmental and organisational practice conducted at step two.

In *In Search of Excellence* (1982) Peters and Waterman identified employees' basic needs as including:

- the need for meaning
- the need for control
- the need for positive reinforcement

In negotiating and agreeing objectives all these needs can be satisfied. The need for meaning can be satisfied by a clear understanding of the relation between individual and organisational targets. The need for control is satisfied by the clarity acquired through discussion of targets and priorities. Positive reinforcement is secured through the satisfaction of meeting agreed success criteria.

Every individual will be involved in the setting of his or her individual objectives. Most individuals will also be involved in the setting of team and departmental objectives. This will ensure that these objectives have meaning for individuals and that they are more likely to be achieved.

Your support, and the support of senior management, needs to be visible and practical throughout this process. You and your team might:

- drop in on objective-setting meetings
- field reports on departmental and managerial objectives
- comment on reports as an agenda item at board meetings
- ensure managerial appraisals consider objective-setting skills.

You and your senior management can usefully set the pace by identifying and publicising organisational objectives.

Harnessing creativity

Another reason for involving everyone is to harness their ideas. Few people do not have good ideas about how they might improve on the way in which their job is done, or on how the organisation might more generally improve its practice. These ideas might be simple or complex, based on experience or simply on reflection.

All too often these ideas are shared with partners and friends, but not with the organisation. In setting your objectives you have the ideal opportunity to solicit these ideas from employees.

GETTING IT RIGHT

A good objective is:

- achievable
- stretching
- honest
- balanced
- meaningful
- measurable
- finite.

Ensuring achievability

> Bill hadn't met his sales targets. He was bored by the job (after ten years of success). Bill's manager was aware of this and of the affection and regard Bill's customers had for him. Perhaps all he needed was a new challenge? To Bill's surprise his appraisal was enormously helpful. He and his manager agreed that a training responsibility might re-awaken his enthusiasm. A training course was identified and, on completion, Bill was accompanied twice a week by a trainee. Success criteria ensured Bill knew what he was supposed to be doing and what would count as evidence of success. Bill exceeded his next sales targets. His trainees think he's brilliant.

To be achievable objectives must be an accurate reflection of an individual's:

- capabilities
- potential
- motivation
- level of support.

If achieving objectives depends on an inflated or otherwise unrealistic assessment of any one of these the objectives will not be met. This leads to loss of self-esteem. Achievable objectives motivate. Unachievable ones demotivate.

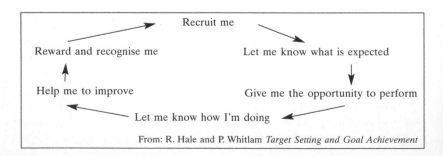

From: R. Hale and P. Whitlam *Target Setting and Goal Achievement*

It is important to be realistic about the support available to those who must meet the objectives set. If someone has been prevented from meeting their objectives through no fault of their own, this can result in the sense of an injustice having been done.

The need to consider such issues shows that steps three and four of the six step process are not entirely independent of each other. In setting objectives it is important to consider how these objectives might be met.

Ensuring stretch
An objective that is too easy to meet is a bad objective. There will be no improvement in performance unless a person is taken out of his or her 'comfort zone'. Yet the point of objectives is improved performance.

In being asked to push harder a person is being offered the opportunity to succeed. Success brings self-esteem. Setting objectives that are both achievable and stretching is the best way to improve organisational morale. Happy people make for happy organisations.

Encouraging honesty
It can be tempting to try to impress others by setting high objectives. This says 'look at us and what we're capable of!' Sometimes people engaging in self-deception do not realise they are being dishonest in the setting of objectives.

But if targets aren't honest, they are unlikely to be met. Worse it might become tempting to 'meet' them by massaging the figures or engaging in wholesale denial. Dishonesty breeds dishonesty.

It is possible to improve performance only in the context of an honest assessment of strengths and weaknesses. It is not possible to raise morale, for example, by setting objectives the achievement of which would be possible only if morale were high. Better to face the truth and set yourself the target of raising morale by setting targets that can be achieved.

This problem can be especially troublesome in a culture of ever-present optimism, where the explicit recognition of potential barriers is seen as unacceptable pessimism. Make sure yours is not such a culture by the explicit and honest discussion of weaknesses and barriers as well as strengths and opportunities.

Setting balanced objectives
It is important to strike a balance between objectives. Every value sets a goal that constrains the pursuit of other goals. Concrete objec-

tives need to be set with an eye to consistency.

Such checks will ensure that no part of the organisation is unwittingly undermining the objectives of another part. Examples of what you want to avoid include:

- Production targets that can be met only by threatening relationships with suppliers and destroying the morale of the production team.
- Individual development targets for teachers that cannot be met consistently with achieving departmental targets.
- Objectives for reducing waiting lists that can be met only if staff ignore the hospital policy of always listening to patients.

Securing meaning

A target that is imposed from above is a target that will not have meaning. To be meaningful targets must be negotiated and agreed so they are fully understood and accepted by the person who has to meet them.

Ideally objectives should be win-win; such that meeting them will benefit individual *and* organisation. If this is not possible it is important to ensure that the packages of objectives to be met by individuals achieve an appropriate balance between benefits to individual and organisation.

Deciding success criteria

If it is unclear what it would be to meet an objective, the objective is unlikely to guide behaviour in any meaningful way. This can be avoided by agreeing success criteria as the objectives are set.

If the objectives set can be quantified in some way, this makes it easy to set success criteria. Examples of such criteria include the following:

- move ten places up the league table
- increase sales by 20 per cent
- decrease customer complaints by 50 per cent
- increase applications by ten per cent
- answer telephones by the fourth ring
- respond to applications within five working days
- decrease errors by 70 per cent.

Not every target can be measured in this way. Indeed some of the most important objectives are not so measurable. It is notoriously difficult, for example, to measure personal development or indeed initiatives by which to improve organisational culture.

Even here, however, careful thought will suggest the criteria by which success can be evaluated. How, after all, do you know there is a problem that needs to be solved if you don't know what counts as evidence for the existence of the problem? And if you can identify the evidence that signals the existence of a problem it is but a short step to identify the evidence that would signal a solution. (It might consist in little more than the disappearance of the evidence for the problem.)

All the examples of objectiveness offered on page 72 included success criteria. Here are some more examples:

Role	Objective	Method of achieving	Success criteria
Secretarial	Improve filing system	Ensure all documents are correctly filed within 24 hours of receipt.	No piles of files lying around in the office. Correct files can be found within minutes of initiating search.
Managerial	Improve communication skills	Attend course, practice during interviews, presentations *etc*	Confidence in communication skills, improvement measured in evaluations from peers and people managed

The success criteria agreed will make it much easier to monitor progress and evaluate success at step five (see Chapter 7).

Setting finite objectives

Part of deciding the criteria for success will involve deciding a timetable for achievement. Either the time limit can be set first (so in setting the success criteria one is asking what sort of improvements it could be realistic to expect in that time). Or the success criteria can be set first (and then a realistic timescale agreed).

Either way the timetable for meeting the objectives must be finite or the objectives will be meaningless.

IDENTIFYING OBJECTIVES

In taking steps one and two you have already started the process by which objectives can be defined. The process is as follows:

- identify your goals (step one)
- identify your baseline (step two)
- decide what needs to be done to close the gap
- agree on what should count as success.

As we saw above this needs to be done at every level: the organisation itself, departments, teams, individuals.

Clearly at each stage of the hierarchy objectives will depend on the objectives of the next level up. It is sensible, therefore, to adopt a top-down process for the setting of objectives.

Here is an example of how objectives at each level might look:

1. **Organisational objectives** – by July 2001 be ready to implement 360° appraisal throughout the organisation. **Success criteria:** Employees at every level have been trained, they understand the benefits of appraisal and the role they will play. Everyone knows when they will be appraised. Knowledge and understanding to be checked by a survey of employees.
2. **Managerial objectives** – by November 2000 to be confident about conducting appraisals and being appraised. **Success criteria:** I have conducted at least four appraisals, gathered mainly positive feedback and identified any further training needs. I have prepared for my own appraisal by identifying possible objectives and appropriate success criteria.
3. **Departmental objectives** – by November 2000 to have devised a workable timetable for appraisal and set up appropriate administrative support. **Success criteria:** The existence of a timetable and an administrative system that have been checked as acceptable by experts and within the department.
4. **Team objectives** – by February 2001 to have fully integrated e-commerce into our marketing strategy. **Success criteria:** we have been fully trained in e-commerce and can outline its benefits, possible problems and solutions. We have revised our marketing strategy to reflect those benefits and avoid those problems.
5. **Individual objectives** – by my next appraisal interview to have improved my presentation skills. **Success criteria:** I have undergone training, given (and received increasingly positive feedback on) at least three presentations and identified further training needs if any.

The process of setting objectives depends on the process of reflection. It is only by taking the time to reflect on our goals (organisational, departmental and individual), on what it would be to achieve these goals and on how we're going to achieve them, that we are likely to succeed in achieving them.

Acquiring a sound understanding

Our daily lives are so busy that it is easy for reflection time to be squeezed out. Yet if we want to succeed we must exercise self-discipline in taking the time to reflect on our goals and our strategies for achieving them. When an organisation:

- takes the time to set its own objectives
- insists that departments and individuals also set objectives
- gives its full support to such a process by providing the time and resources necessary

it is recognising the importance of such reflection.

Prêt à Manger is a relatively new and phenomenally successful chain of sandwich shops. They have a very clear mission statement that appears on all the organisation's literature and on the front window of every outlet. When staff join Prêt à Manger they join an induction programme that introduces them to the Prêt vision: the programme involves reflecting on the words used to express the vision, their meaning and the reason that the qualities they express are important. Employees are encouraged to put themselves into the position of customers who care about what they eat and what they buy their families so that they can feel for themselves the importance of Prêt's values. It is this conscious striving to understand and live up to its values, combined with the sort of working practices that underline the value Prêt places on employees, that is believed by director Julian Metcalfe to be the source of Prêt's success.

You will already have provided much of the time needed for reflection if:

- At step one, everyone was involved in deciding on the organisational mission.
- The induction process makes sure that every new recruit is required to reflect on the organisation's mission and what it means to them.
- At step two everyone was involved in reflecting on current practice, identifying success and failures.

If such is the case people will already have a sound understanding of the organisational mission and of current strengths and weaknesses.

At step three such people need only:

- crystallise their understanding of where they might improve/agree on success criteria.

Examples of organisational objectives include:

- Improve internal communication systems by developing the intranet and training all staff in the use of email.
- Improve customer service by conducting a survey to discover customer needs and by acting to fulfil those needs.
- Improve facilities for staff by extending and redecorating the staff canteen, constructing surveys into food preferences, providing a changing menu with an extended choice.
- Conduct a cost-benefit analysis into the introduction of flexi-time by visiting companies who have introduced it and conducting a staff survey into likely usage.

At step four we shall be considering the steps that need to be taken to ensure that objectives are met.

Organisational clarity

Steps one and two together constitute a process of clarification. Once they are complete the organisation, its departments, teams and individuals should all have a firm grasp of:

- their goals
- how their goals fit into each context
- how their goals relate to each other
- the extent to which they are achieving their goals.

Such clarity can usefully form the basis of a written description of each task, function and role within the organisation. In reflecting, for example, on his or her own role within the organisation and his or her own objectives, an individual will be well-placed to write a description of:

- his or her own role within the organisation
- the daily tasks that go into that role

- the relations with others that support that role
- the skills and competencies needed to fulfil the role
- the role-objectives to be met.

Such descriptions can be enormously useful if a person is off sick, on holiday, undergoing training or otherwise not available to do their job. It is also useful, of course, when the person moves on and must be replaced.

Similar descriptions can be written for departments and for teams. These can be useful for the purposes of the induction of new recruits and those who move within the organisation.

SUMMARY

In this chapter we have discussed step three, the process of identifying concrete and achievable objectives for:

- the organisation itself
- organisational departments and teams
- individuals.

Deriving such objectives requires people at every level to acquire a practical understanding of the organisational mission and departmental objectives. In acquiring such understanding people come to understand the contribution they make in a way that underpins confidence in their role, clarity of focus and a commitment to success.

It is in taking step three that the mission statement stops being simply a string of 'feel good' nouns. It is now poised to become engaged in every aspect of the behaviour of the organisation.

6

Step Four: Planning Change

Change: the act or instance of making or becoming different.

Having completed step three you have:

* Identified the organisational mission; the organisation's aims and values.
* Reviewed current practice in relation to these aims and values.
* Set concrete organisational, departmental, team and individual objectives.
* Identified what will count as success in each case.
* Identified times by which each objective must be achieved.

You can now formulate plans of action by which to satisfy the success criteria for each objective in the time permitted.

WRITING YOUR ACTION PLAN

In formulating action plans it is necessary to rehearse, in your imagination (and where appropriate in discussion) every part of the achievement of your objective, the problems you might face, how you'll overcome them and the resources you'll need.

This will enable you to:

* Identify each element of your plan.

* Reflect on how each element can be achieved.

* Ensure the achievement of all elements will result in success.

* Anticipate problems and prepare responses.

* Get right the timing of each element and of the whole.

* Assign responsibility for the success of each element.

* Identify necessary resources for each part of your plan.

Insofar as everyone in the organisation has agreed objectives, everyone in the organisation will be involved in this step.

The complexity of this task will depend, of course, on the type of objective to be met. However simple the objective, its successful achievement will depend on proper planning.

ANALYSING OBJECTIVES

In formulating an action plan the best starting point is an analysis of each objective. This involves breaking down each of your objectives into the sub-objectives that you will need to achieve in order to achieve the objective itself.

Such sub-objectives might include:

- the gathering of relevant information
- undergoing some training or arranging for others to do so
- consulting outside experts
- deciding between different approaches
- consulting stakeholders for their views
- securing commitment from stakeholders.

In Table 1 we can see an illustration of how an

expanded organisational mission statement ...
has generated ...   **departmental objectives ...**
from which has been derived a number of ...
sub-objectives.

These sub-objectives are severally necessary and jointly sufficient for the successful achievement of the stated departmental goal.

You will want to agree success criteria for each sub-objective to ensure that you will know what counts as evidence for its achievement. You might (will almost certainly) find that the sub-objectives you have identified can be further broken down into sub-sub-objectives.

Table 2 shows an illustration.

Expanded mission statement	Human Resources departmental objective	Sub-objectives
Actively work with employees to enable them to give of their best	To introduce an organisation-wide appraisal scheme by which to work with employees to identify individual training and development needs. **Success criteria** One scheme has been chosen from a field of at least three. There are clear reasons for choosing that scheme over the others. All managers have been trained in the required techniques. All employees are aware of the scheme and understand the benefits. A timetable for appraisal has been set up throughout the organisation. **Completion time: 02.05.01**	1. Conduct research into at least three different appraisal schemes. 2. Identify potential barriers to appraisal by conducting a survey into management and non-management attitudes. 3. Choose the best scheme in consultation with representatives from across the organisation. 4. Use newsletters, noticeboards, suggestion boxes and departmental awayadays to keep staff informed and invite comments. 5. Conduct a small pilot. 6. Assuming success of pilot, identify training requirements and how they might be met. 7. Continue to keep staff informed and invite comments. 8. Set up training timetable. 9. Devise organisation-wide timetable for appraisal in consultation with departments. 10. Launch scheme.

Table 1.   Objectives and sub-objectives.

Expanded mission statement	Human Resources departmental objective	Sub-objectives	Sub-sub-objectives
Actively work with employees to enable them to give of their best	To introduce an organisation-wide appraisal scheme by which to work with individual training and development needs. **Success criteria** One scheme has been chosen from a field of at least three. There are clear reasons for choosing that scheme over the others. All managers have been trained in the required techniques. All employees are aware of the scheme and understand its benefits. A timetable for appraisal has been set up throughout the organisation. **Completion time** 02.05.01	1. Conduct research into at least three different appraisal schemes. 2. Identify potential barriers to appraisal by conducting a survey into management and non-management attitudes. 3. Choose one scheme in consultation with representatives from across the organisation. 4. Throughout the process keep staff informed and invite comments. 5. Conduct a small pilot. 6. Assuming success of pilot, identify training requirements and how they might be met. 7. Continue to keep staff informed and invite comments. 8. Set up training timetable. 9. Devise organisation-wide timetable for appraisal in consultation with departments. 10. Launch scheme.	(1a) Identify useful books, articles. (1b) Consult outside experts. (1c) Visit other organisations with successful schemes. (2 and 3a) Decide who to consult, how and which information we need. (4a) Speak to union representatives, write regular up date for newsletter, put notices on staff boards, use suggestion boxes. (5a) Choose individuals to appraise during pilot and to undergo appraisal. Ensure they are truly representative. (5b) Agree a timetable. Decide how the pilot should be evaluated. (6 and 7a) Decide who should be trained, by whom, when, how and where. (8a) Gather information about who should be appraised and who will do the appraising. Collect departmental timetables Devise matchings and timetable. (9a) Press launch and party for staff.

Table 2.   Breaking down sub-objectives.

AGREEING A TIMESCALE

Armed with a firm grasp of each of the actions you will need to take you will want to draft a 'timeline' to ensure that you meet your objective within the timescale allowed.

Clearly you must allow yourself enough time to complete each element of the plan, including those whose completion depends on the prior completion of other parts. Equally clearly you need to leave enough time for each elements of your plan whilst still completing your plan by the time limit allowed for the achievement of the overall objective.

Table 3 shows a timeline for our imaginary example.

Securing flexibility

It is important that in formulating your action plans and deciding your timeline you are flexible. There's many a slip twixt cup and lip, and you need to be flexible enough to deal with such slips as they arise. Timelines should never be so tight that they are completely thrown out by something going wrong.

You will, of course, have tried to anticipate the various things that might go wrong, but you would be wise nevertheless to assume that you might not have succeeded in predicting everything.

Because you will have built this flexibility into your timetable you will need to review and revise your timeline as you achieve your sub-objectives (and your sub-sub-objectives). If you *have* succeeded in anticipating problems you might find you can bring things forward (or do something in addition to what you have already done or to a better standard than you thought would be possible). If you haven't you may need to take advantage of the built-in flexibility and re-arrange your timings.

In constructing your timeline you will find it useful to schedule meetings at which to discuss progress. This is discussed further at step five (Chapter 7).

ASSIGNING RESPONSIBILITY

When objectives (and sub-objectives) are to be met, it is always a good idea to assign responsibility for their successful achievement to a named individual.

Although no one individual is likely to be able to achieve the objective by themselves, anything for which *everyone* is responsible becomes something that is *no one*'s responsibility. And something that is no one's responsibility will not get done.

Expanded mission statement	Human Resources objectve	Sub-objectives	time-line	sub-sub-objectives	time-line
Actively work with employees to enable them to give of their best.	To introduce an organisation-wide appraisal scheme by which to work with employees to identify individual training and development needs. Jane Doe (Head of HR) **Success criteria** One scheme has been chosen from a field of at least three. There are clear reasons for choosing that scheme over the others. All managers have been trained in the required techniques. All employees are aware of the scheme and understand its benefits. A timetable for appraisal has been set up throughout the organisation. **Completion time** 02.05.01	1. Conduct research into at least three different appraisal schemes. (James Smith) 2. Identify potential barriers by conducting a survey into management and non-management attitudes. (Annette Jay) 3. Choose one scheme in consultation across the organisation. (JD, JS & AJ) 4. Throughout the process keep staff informed and invite comments. (AJ & Rob Nott) 5. Conduct a small pilot. (JS and AJ) 6. Assuming success of pilot, identify training requirements and how they might be met. (JS, AJ & RN) 7. Set up training timetable. (JS, AJ & RN) 8. Devise organisation-wide timetable for appraisal in consultation with departments. (AJ & Pete Ng) 9. Launch scheme.	by Mar 2000 by Mar 2000 by June 2000 by Dec 2000 by Feb 2001 by Feb 2001 by Apr 2001 May 2001	(1a) Identify useful books, articles. (Mary Jones) (1b) Read books *etc* and consult outside experts. (JS) (1c) Visit other organisations with successful schemes. (JS) (2 and 3a) Decide who to consult, how and which information we need. (JS & AJ) (4a) Speak to union representatives, write regular up-date for newsletter, put notices on staff boards, use suggestion boxes. (AJ & RN) (5c) Choose individuals to appraise and undergo appraisal during pilot. Ensure they are truly representative. Agree a timetable. Decide how the pilot should be evaluated. (JS, AJ & RN) (6 and 7a) Decide who should be trained, by whom, when, how and where. (JS, AJ & RN) (8a) Gather information about who should be appraised and who will do the appraising. Collect departmental timetables. Devise matchings and timetable. (JS, AJ & RN) (9a) Press launch and party for staff. (All)	Now by Feb 2000 by Mar 2000 by Mar 2000 by June 2000 by Jan 2001 by Apr 2001 May 2001

Table 3.   Introducing a timeline.

The best way to assign responsibility for the achievement of an objective is to make the identification of the responsible person part of your planning.

Once identified this person's initials should be included in the plan of action and the achievement of objective included amongst that person's personal objectives.

You will see in the example above that names or initials have been appended to every element of the action plan. This ensures that that person will be held accountable for the successful completion, by the required date, of that element of the plan.

IDENTIFYING NECESSARY RESOURCES

The successful achievement of some parts of the plan will require only time and energy. Other parts of the plan will require the cooperation of others. Still other parts will depend on money, space, equipment, expertise and/or other resources.

It is important that these resources be identified as part of the planning. The securing of them should also be part of the plan. The non-availability at the appropriate time of the appropriate resources can scupper even the best laid plans.

The resources required should be reviewed and revised whenever the plan itself is reviewed and revised. The need for resources will clearly have implications for organisational and departmental budgets. These implications need to be considered as plans are made.

There may also be implications for the use of available space and/or equipment. If, for example, there is only one or a restricted number of large rooms available for big gatherings and such a gathering is part of your plan, then you will need to secure one of these rooms as early as possible. If you have no large rooms at all then part of your planning must involve the finding of such a room.

You might want to add to your timeline a column listing the resources you need, together with the initials of the person responsible for securing them and the time by which they must be secured (*ie* the time they must be *booked*, not the time they are *needed*).

COORDINATING CHANGE

Before any action plan is finalised it would be a good idea for it to be checked to ensure that each of the proposed actions are:

- consistent with each of the goals outlined in the expanded mission statement

- not needlessly duplicating the planned actions of other departments and of the organisation as a whole.

Such final checks can help to ensure that organisational practice remains coherent over the necessary period of change.

SUMMARY

During steps one to three you have identified the organisational mission in such a way that everyone understands it. You have conducted a review to determine the extent to which you are successfully achieving that mission. In conducting this review you will also have been able to identify opportunities for improvement.

On the basis of this, at step three, you (and your departments, teams and individuals) identified various objectives the achievement of which will enable you to improve performance, the better to achieve the organisational mission. Success criteria for the achievement of these objectives have been agreed, as have the times by which they must be achieved.

At step four everyone is involved in formulating plans by which these objectives can be achieved within the time allowed. These plans enable practical sense to be made of these objectives. The planning involves:

- identifying the different actions that need to be taken

- ensuring that taken together these add up to success

- anticipating problems and preparing responses

- getting your timing right

- assigning responsibility for success

- identifying and securing the necessary resources.

You know your goals and you have in place strategies by which to achieve these goals. The time has come to consider how you will monitor your achievement and evaluate your success.

In doing this you will be gathering the evidence you need to be sure that your strategies are succeeding in helping you to achieve your goals.

7

Step Five: Monitoring Progress and Evaluating Success

To monitor: to maintain surveillance.
To evaluate: to assess performance.

Having set objectives and decided on the strategies by which you will achieve these objectives, you will now want to set up systems by which to:

* monitor the success of your strategies in achieving your goals
* evaluate your success in achieving your goals.

In this chapter we shall discuss ways in which systems of monitoring and evaluation can be used to:

* underpin confidence in good performance
* give warning of poor performance
* identify practice on which to build
* identify practice that should be changed.

MONITORING PROGRESS

Monitoring progress involves the effective use of systems, procedures and processes that enable you to be sure of the smooth running of the action plans designed at step four. Such systems, procedures and processes, used properly, will give you:

* warning of the need to review and revise such plans
* the confidence of knowing when things are going well
* evidence (if you need it) to justify the changes you are making.

In monitoring your progress you will be helping yourself to avoid nasty surprises and to maintain control of your attempts to achieve your goals.

EVALUATING SUCCESS

To evaluate success is to take time, after your goals have successfully been achieved, to analyse your achievement of these goals. During such 'debriefings' you will be reflecting on what you have done well. You will also be reflecting on the things that might have been done better.

In each case your aim is explicitly to identify the lessons you might learn to guide future behaviour. Such debriefings will allow you to build on your successes and learn from your mistakes.

INVOLVING EVERYONE

Unsurprisingly everyone should be involved in the process of monitoring performance. At the very least they will be involved in:

- monitoring their own progress towards their own goals

- getting and giving feedback on the contribution they are making to departmental, team and organisational progress.

You and your senior management team will, of course, be involved in monitoring progress and evaluating success at every level. You (and they) will be involved in:

- monitoring progress towards your personal objectives
- evaluating your successful achievement of these objectives
- monitoring progress towards organisational objectives
- evaluating the successful achievement of organisational objectives.

The successful monitoring of organisational progress and the successful evaluation of organisational objectives will, of course, involve an understanding of departmental contributions to progress and success.

This will inevitably require you to follow the progress of departments, key teams and key individuals. This may involve simply gathering 'headline results' from the departments, teams and individuals involved (in the form, for example, of reports). Or you may choose actively to involve yourself in the systems, procedures and processes adopted by teams, departments and individuals.

Certainly you should be involved in monitoring the progress and evaluating the success of senior management.

LINKING STEPS FOUR AND FIVE

At step four, in planning strategies for achieving goals, part of the process was deciding on:

- the criteria by which success would be judged
- the time by which the goal would be achieved
- the times by which important steps to that goal would be achieved.

The timetable agreed at step four will determine when the time has come to evaluate success. It will also suggest a useful timetable for monitoring progress.

Progress needs to be monitored in such a way that there is plenty of time to act, should action prove necessary. In some cases progress can and should continually be monitored. In other cases checks – *eg* meetings at which progress reports are given – need to be built into the timetable.

Success, on the other hand, can only be evaluated once the time for achieving the goal has been reached. Indeed it is often sensible to allow some time to have elapsed after the time for achieving the goal has been reached. The purpose of such evaluation is to guide future action in the light of both success and failures. Such successes and failures are not always apparent at the time of achievement. It is often only once things have settled that we are in a position to make a true evaluation.

The best way to underline the importance of step five is to consider, at step four, how and when progress will be assessed.

CHOOSING YOUR METHODS

In deciding how you are going to monitor progress and evaluate success you need to consider the success criteria you identified at step three.

If, for example, one of your aims is to reduce absenteeism by 30 per cent then you will need to find some way of measuring absenteeism and you will need to monitor its levels. This will ensure that as time moves on towards the date at which you must have achieved your objective, you are in a position to know whether levels are:

- going down
- going down at a rate consistent with achieving your objective.

Such systems might include:

- 'clocking on'

- signing in

- taking of registers by administrative staff

- regular checking of the figure generated by such systems.

Levels could be checked at two-monthly or quarterly intervals.

If one of your sub-objectives is to discover *why* people are absent (physical illness, stress, family responsibilities...), the better to remove the causes of absenteeism, then you will need systems to gather qualitative data. These might include:

- questionnaires to be completed by absentees on their return to work

- interviews to be conducted with returners

- interviews conducted with those who are frequently absent.

Clearly you are not going to gather much useful data if the people to whom you talk are afraid that by being honest they are likely to be punished.

You might consider an 'amnesty' for those who admit to malingering in return for information about why they malinger and what might stop them. If you find that a significant number of employees absent themselves for reasons of stress, for example, you will need to take steps to reduce stress. If they absent themselves to deal with family responsibilities different approaches are called for. (If it is simply malingering, a quite different approach will be needed.)

Alternatively you might consider conducting a survey of all employees in which none needs give their name or department. Another method would be to conduct a survey into (*eg* employees' family responsibilities) including questions about whether and under what circumstances employees feel they need to take unauthorised absence to deal with such responsibilities.

You will also need to make decisions about how to monitor progress towards a qualitative objectives such as the improvement of presentation skills.

In monitoring progress towards such goals you might:

- record 'baseline' data
- record similar data as the person undergoes extra training and acquires more confidence.

Such data can only come from those to whom the person in question has given a presentation. In keeping with step five you might want to arrange that all organisational presentations are evaluated by those to whom the presentation was given.

Such evaluations might comprise questionnaires, to be completed at the end of the presentation. These should include questions on:

1. The content of the presentation (points made, logical ordering, importance, relevance to audience).
2. The way the content was presented (enthusiasm, clarity, audibility).
3. The use of audio-visual aids (overheads, slides, microphones used well and appropriately).
4. The use of figures and statistics (for their own sake, to illustrate important points, to underline arguments).
5. Body language (arm waving, hiding behind notes, pacing).

And in each case you should try to gather quantitative data (including scales of 1–5 where 5 is excellent and 1 is poor) and qualitative data (give reasons for your answer . . .).

If such data is available it should become relatively easy to detect an improvement over time (or indeed a lack of improvement). In the absence of such data detecting such improvements becomes difficult if not impossible.

Similar systems would be appropriate for most qualitative objectives.

MAKING USE OF APPRAISAL

One of the most important means of monitoring progress and evaluating success is appraisal. The setting up of an appraisal system involves the setting up of a regular cycle of meetings for everyone in the organisation (including you). These meetings involve the person to be appraised and the person (or occasionally persons) doing the appraising.

At these meetings:

• performance is reviewed

• career plans are discussed

• objectives (personal and organisational) are set

• success criteria are identified

• decisions are made about how progress might be monitored

- possible plans of action are discussed
- timetables are negotiated
- problems are anticipated and resolutions suggested.

Importantly appraisal should be seen as a means of support to the person being appraised. The idea is that in being appraised a person, with the help of another, can take stock and make plans for their own development, both career-wise and personally (if appropriate). Appraisal can provide one of the main vehicles for the six step process as it pertains to individuals. The implementation of a good appraisal system is a concrete expression of the way in which the organisation values each of its employees as individuals.

The idea of appraisal being a source of support ensures that appraisal should not be too closely linked to systems of recognition and reward. It is vital that in appraisal people take an honest look at themselves and their own progress. If they believe that the admission of weaknesses might negatively affect their remuneration or prospects of promotion they are much less likely to be honest.

If people come to see that the admission of weaknesses leads to useful advice and practical support in the attempt to eliminate these weaknesses they will be far less inclined to exaggerate their strengths.

Although Prêt à Manger has a system of regular appraisals (an informal cup of coffee in a nearby cafe), the organisation believes that each of its team leaders should spend much of his time monitoring and evaluating staff performance. Staff appraisal cannot, the organisation believes, be done to a timetable; it has to be a constant process of recognising both when a team member is doing well and when that team member is not doing well. The constant feedback from this process enables team members to adjust their behaviour whenever necessary (and gives them a glow of pride when they're doing well).

Part of creating this trust will be building the relationship between appraiser and appraisee. If the latter comes to see the former as a mentor rather than a judge the appraisal is likely to be useful.

The role of mentor involves helping appraisees objectively to:

- evaluate their own performance
- identify their strengths and weaknesses
- improve performance by setting appropriate objectives

- monitor their own performance

- evaluate their own success.

The word 'objectively' is important here. The appraisal system depends heavily on other systems, procedures and processes for monitoring progress. Appraisal can only be useful if systems such as those mentioned above are set up, taken seriously throughout the organisation and used as the basis for appraisal.

Systems for monitoring progress and evaluating success (including systems of appraisal) will be taken seriously only if:

1. You and other members of the management team are visibly involved (*eg* in being appraised, gathering the results of other forms of monitoring and interested in evaluations).
2. People have been properly trained in the techniques needed effectively to understand and use the monitoring systems, procedures and processes agreed.
3. The time and resources needed for properly implementing systems, procedures and processes (including appraisal) are ring fenced.
4. Timetables for appraisal should not overload management – appraisals need to be staggered throughout the year if each person is to get the attention they deserve.
5. Appraisers and appraisees prepare properly for appraisal by gathering the information they need, reflecting on their goals, strengths and weaknesses and on plans by which they might achieve these goals, build on these strengths and eliminate their weaknesses.

The information on which appraisal is based should not all come from 'above'. Only a '360° appraisal' can give anything like an objective picture of someone's performance. Pupils, therefore, and support staff should be involved in the appraisal of teachers; patients, nurses and porters in the appraisal of doctors; administrative and post-room staff in the appraisal of managers. Such information can sensitively be gathered by questionnaires and in interviews.

WHISTLE-BLOWING

A system that it is particularly important to put in place is one that enables people to express their concerns about organisational bad practice.

There is rarely a disaster when we don't hear afterwards from employees who were already concerned about the bad practice that led to the disaster. Why, you might ask, did they not express their concerns within?

Well, there are lots of reasons. Here are a few:

- fear of what others would think

- desire to be seen in a certain way

- fear of being silly (or of others believing we're silly)

- fear of being sacked

- fear of hurting others

- loyalty to colleagues or bosses

- desire that others should like us.

Occasionally employees who feel like this 'blow the whistle' on their organisation. In such cases, concern about what is going on, combined with frustration with the belief they won't be heard sympathetically within the organisation, causes employees officially to express their concerns to those outside.

All well and good if it involves a potential disaster or if the organisation's actions are immoral or illegal, but such whistle-blowing can leave the reputation of the organisation in shreds.

Anaesthetist Stephen Bolsin became a professional outcast when he questioned colleagues' operating techniques after the deaths of 29 infants. Barings Bank was wiped out after it ignored a director's warnings about lax systems. Paul van Buitenen, a Dutch auditor, blew the whistle on corruption in the European Parliament, but was suspended for doing so. Perhaps if a system had been in place by which train drivers could express concern about going through red lights, the Ladbroke Grove accident would never have happened?

Does your organisation ignore or punish people who share their concerns? Might this force them to 'blow the whistle' in public. Are you certain there is no organisational practice that could lead to this? Could your organisation survive the loss of reputation this could involve? Would it be worth your reviewing provision for the expression of serious concerns?

If you are going through the six step process you will probably not be an organisation in which people are afraid openly to express their concerns. But it is simply not possible to eliminate all the factors that prevent people from sharing concerns with those within. It would be sensible, therefore, to put in place systems that enable people to share concerns without identifying themselves.

You as Chief Executive might make it clear to people that you are always happy to receive letters from people, anonymously if necessary. You might put suggestion boxes in corridors, lavatories and anywhere out of the way. You might invite comments for anonymous publication in the newsletter.

You might also instigate systems according to which those who share concerns are publicly rewarded. Certainly you should take steps to eliminate 'punishments' for such behaviour.

TROUBLESHOOTING

It is possible in setting up effective monitoring systems to anticipate some common problems. These include problems to do with:

- accountability bringing blame
- unsatisfactory documentation
- monitoring and evaluation for its own sake
- concerns about objectivity and subjectivity
- confrontation and disagreement
- distorting beliefs.

Accountability bringing blame

It is important in monitoring progress and evaluating success that the systems introduced are not seen as delivering only bad news. This is especially important in appraisal. We can learn from what we do well as well as from what we do badly. And we should work at building our strengths as well as eliminating our weaknesses.

Human beings have a tendency only to hear bad news. The person whose evaluation sheets show that 20 people thought their presentation was excellent and two thought it was awful will often remember the two more clearly than they remember the 20.

This can ensure that accountability brings with it a culture of blame. And this can undermine the sort of trust that grounds good relationships. It is extremely important that people do not think that you are monitoring their progress in order simply to identify, and blame them for, their shortcomings.

If they think this the energy you put into monitoring progress and evaluating success might be counter-productive in destroying relationships throughout the organisation.

The way to avoid this problem is to educate people. Everyone needs to know that their performance is being monitored for their benefit as much as for the benefit of the organisation. They also need to see that the system will generate good news as readily as it generates bad news: if they do something well, it will be recognised and, where appropriate, rewarded.

Unsatisfactory documentation

Sometimes the documentation used for monitoring performance is designed in such a way that the only information the system *can* deliver is bad.

If, for example, an evaluation sheet only has boxes for 'satisfactory' 'unsatisfactory' and 'poor' the person being evaluated has reason to complain. There is no possibility here of excellence being recorded: the best that can be recorded is 'satisfactory'. People can be forgiven for feeling it simply isn't worth putting in the effort if the most they can be recognised for is being 'satisfactory'.

Monitoring and evaluation for its own sake

There is no point in setting up systems to monitor things in which no one is interested. Nor is there any point in monitoring a behaviour that cannot be changed. And if more is spent monitoring a system than can possibly be justified by the system being monitored, there is little purpose in the exercise. Here are the conditions under which monitoring systems are worth setting up:

- there is a clear set of success criteria (either quantitative or qualitative)
- the evidence generated by the system is potentially useful (in changing behaviour, providing evidence for success, making plans)
- there are people who want or need to know the results.

If one or more of these conditions isn't satisfied then you will be wasting your time in setting up a system for monitoring progress.

Concerns about objectivity and subjectivity

It is important not to concentrate exclusively on quantitative measurements. The fact that something cannot be measured quantitatively does not mean it is less valuable. Such a view will lead to our valuing only what is measurable (quantitatively), not measuring what is valuable (perhaps qualitatively).

One of the reasons that people can value quantitative measures over qualitative is that quantitative measures seem more 'objective' in that they don't rely on anyone's feelings or opinions. Qualitative measurements attempt to draw conclusions from what people say about what they think or feel. Some people think this is simply unscientific.

But this is a distortion of the importance of science. (It is also a misunderstanding of science.) The idea that we might somehow get by without trying to understand others' thoughts and feelings is a nonsense. Our ability, through what we say and do, to communicate our feelings, beliefs, emotions and sensations and to understand those communicated by others underpins all our interactions. It grounds our ability to:

- manage others
- cooperate and collaborate
- care for others
- teach and learn
- listen successfully
- inspire, enthuse and engage.

Scientists, given their need for collaboration, need to engage in such practices as much as anyone else (and far more, in fact, than the artist or philosopher who works alone in the garret).

If we want to 'measure' things like morale and reputation we are going to have to communicate effectively with others and try our best to understand them when they communicate with us.

Such 'subjective' assessment can be made more objective by gathering the views of many people. This is why questionnaires and large consultations are so important. Intersubjectivity of this kind does not amount to objectivity, but it gets jolly close.

We can of course supplement these 'subjective' measures with methods that do not involve directly asking people about their feelings and attitudes towards their work and their relationships with others. As we have seen we can learn a lot about organisational morale from such things as:

- staff turnover
- sick leave
- application rates
- incidents of bullying/vandalism/abuse
- participation in voluntary organisational activities
- sales levels/exam results/waiting lists *etc.*

Such relatively objective yardsticks are useful indicators of morale. They do not, however, explain themselves. If you want to know *why* staff turnover is so high you will need to ask people about their reasons for leaving. (This was discussed during step two in Chapter 4, see especially page 62.

There are two particularly important forms of worry under this heading that deserve to be dealt with separately.

Confrontation and disagreement

A lot of people worry about appraisal (for example) because they are worried about the possibility of disagreeing with their appraiser (or indeed with the person they are appraising). It is this sort of disagreement that tempts us to say 'it's all subjective'.

Such disagreements will occur and sometimes confrontations will be necessary. This is why, in discussing performance, we use indicators other than our own opinions. If we can point to hard evidence for the belief that someone needs to improve their communication skills, or for the claim that sales figures are down, then there is one less thing to argue about.

This doesn't mean there isn't plenty of scope left for argument and this is why it is so important that appraisers be trained in appraisal techniques and that appraisees understand the potential benefits to them of appraisal.

Distorting beliefs

One of the most important parts of appraisal training deals with the need to be aware of beliefs that can distort an evaluation. There are still people who believe, for example, that women are not as good as men at certain things. Such people are likely to interpret events consistently with this belief to the detriment of women (or men).

Other distorting beliefs include our tendency to see someone who has done something well once as unable to do anything wrong. The flip side of this is a tendency to regard someone who once did badly as likely always to do badly.

And we are all subject to the force of first impressions (a variant of the last mentioned distortion).

A good appraiser will be aware of all the possible distortions to which they are subject. He or she will be prepared to reflect on their own views, scouring them of these distortions with the aim of being fair all round.

SUMMARY

In this chapter we have discussed the importance of setting up systems by which to:

* monitor progress towards achieving the objectives set at step three
* evaluate success in achieving these goals.

Both the monitoring of progress and the evaluation of success depend on the prior identification of objectives, criteria for success in meeting these objectives, a time limit and an action plan for the achievement of these objectives. These were covered at steps two, three and four (Chapters 4, 5 and 6).

In this chapter we have seen that monitoring progress enables us to:

* be confident that objectives are being met, and/or
* get early warning of difficulties.

For this to be possible progress needs to be monitored either continuously or in such a way as to leave time for the review and revision of action plans. Monitoring progress involves setting up systems by which to gather both quantitative and qualitative information.

Evaluating the achievement of objectives, on the other hand, enables us to:

* build on success
* learn from failure.

This is possible only if we take the time to reflect on the achievement (or lack of achievement) of goals after the fact. Evaluating success requires the honest assessment of what has been done badly *and* what has been done well.

In evaluating success it is important to avoid a 'blame culture'. This can be done by ensuring that as much importance is attached to what has been done well as is attached to what has been done badly.

To motivate everyone success, once identified, needs to be recognised and, where appropriate, rewarded. It is to this we turn in the next chapter during our discussion of step six.

8

Step Six: Recognising (and Rewarding) Effort and Achievement

Recognise: to acknowledge someone's existence, validity, character or claims.

Recognition and/or reward reinforces the ownership of success. In making it clear that we are aware of someone's efforts and achievements we validate them and their sense of responsibility for organisational success.

Mutual recognition is an essential condition of effective relationships, it flows from the emotional intelligence that underpins goodwill and liking. In a society in which the acknowledgment of strengths can be deemed immodest, the appropriate reward of others' contributions can be invaluable. It gives people 'permission' to feel pride in their work.

In this chapter we shall conclude our exploration of the six step process by looking at the importance of recognition and reward, and at different ways in which people can be recognised and rewarded.

RECOGNISING OR REWARDING?

It is tempting to think that these are the same thing. But it is possible to:

- embarrass someone by rewarding them when recognition would be more appropriate
- generate resentment by continuing simply to recognise someone when reward would be more appropriate.

To recognise someone is to acknowledge implicitly or explicitly that you are aware of and value their contribution. To reward someone is explicitly to acknowledge someone's contribution by offering a token of appreciation.

Recognition is usually a two way process: good secretaries will make sure their bosses are aware of their triumphs just as good bosses make sure their secretaries know they are appreciated.

> In a survey of 2000 managers 40 per cent cited lack of recognition as the factor most likely to make them quit.
>
> From *The Price of Success*, Ceridian Performance Partners

Reward, on the other hand, tends to be a one way process. The ability to reward somebody for something is usually the prerogative of those higher up the organisational hierarchy or of the organisation itself. (Reward can, indeed, be counterproductive in emphasising imbalances of power.) Reward is appropriate when:

* something has been done
    - that needn't have been done
    - extraordinarily well
    - under difficult circumstances
    - for a long time.

Despite the differences between recognition and reward, the boundary between them is not sharp. A simple 'thank you', for example, can be both recognition and reward. A salary is offered more in recognition for a person's contribution than as a reward for it (yet it feels more like the latter).

VALIDATING OTHERS

Good relationships are a crucial element of organisational success. Good relationships, however, depend on mutual recognition. Everybody, whatever their position, likes to be validated by others: nobody likes to be taken for granted.

Because teamworking depends on good relationships, good teamwork also depends on mutual recognition between team-members. It is this mutual recognition of the contribution of others that leads to the sort of bonding that is a key ingredient of team (departmental and organisational) success.

To the extent that an organisation nurtures the mutual recognition that underpins good relationships it will be nurturing its own chances of success.

Recognition of others can take many forms, including:

* asking for their input

* involving them in decision-making

* including them in activities

- recognising they have a life outside work
- understanding they can't do two things at once
- asking after partners and children
- remembering details of personal conversations
- giving responsibility wherever appropriate
- delegating the interesting stuff too.

The ability to offer recognition of this kind is the part of EQ (**emotional intelligence**) claimed by Professor Daniel Goleman to be a better predictor of success than IQ. The EQ of an organisation will, of course, be a function of the EQ of its members and of the ways its systems and processes nurture that EQ.

EQ is particularly important for management. If managers are encouraged actively to recognise the people they manage, these people will soon find themselves returning the recognition. If managers' ability effectively to recognise the contribution of their staff is included amongst the things for which they are assessed, recognised and where appropriate rewarded, the organisation will soon build for itself a culture where recognition is the norm.

In schools the recognition of teachers' contribution will underpin teachers' recognition of pupils' successes. If someone doesn't themselves feel valued they are unlikely to value others.

The headteacher of a northern secondary school was pleased and touched when, at her last appraisal, her staff made it clear that she was the best head they'd ever worked for. During the appraisal interviews, staff member after staff member had mentioned some incident that had made them feel that the head cared for them as people. One female teacher mentioned the note she'd got when she had to take time off to care for a sick husband. Another mentioned the flowers she received whilst in hospital for breast cancer. A third mentioned the fact that two weeks after a conversation in which he'd mentioned house-moving difficulties, the head had asked how the move was going. Pupils and support staff had similar stories to tell. It was clear to the governors as they conducted the appraisal that under this head the school had become a vibrant and exciting place to work, relationships had improved all round and everyone was keen to give their very best. The governors believe the head's emotional intelligence, her constant recognition of staff as individuals, has made a major contribution to the school's excellent academic record.

The success of such systems requires the sort of 360° appraisal outlined in Chapter 7. It also requires organisational recognition (as well as organisational reward) of management skill in this area. The manager who doesn't feel valued is unlikely to value staff.

When Paul Dacre of Associated Newspapers forgot to mention the subeditors in his speech at the organisation's annual party, each sub arrived the next morning to find a bottle of champagne on their desk.

(Reported in the *Times*)

Clearly the recruitment procedures of an organisation will have a major effect on the organisation's EQ. If, in recruitment, organisations always consciously look for someone with a high EQ (even if the job strictly speaking doesn't demand it) they will eventually improve relationships throughout the organisation.

The organisation can enhance the conditions under which mutual recognition flourishes by:

- providing opportunities for socialising across the organisation

- subsidising pleasant places where people can eat and drink together

- ensuring the working environment is attractive and comfortable

- appointing cheerful and friendly catering and reception staff

- introducing flexible working.

Such things make staff feel valued and staff who feel valued usually also feel loyal and committed.

A busy medical practice conducted a survey of patients and discovered that one of the things they disliked most was having to wait in the cavernous and dingy waiting room. Deciding that something needed to be done all the partners rolled up their sleeves and got busy. They replaced the frosted glass in the windows with clear glass so patients could see into the rather pleasant gardens. They painted the walls a sunny yellow and framed some cheap and cheerful posters for the walls. They begged and borrowed some large house plants and replaced the ancient *Readers' Digests* with back copies of their own magazines and those of the receptionist. Nearly all patients remarked on the changes, saying how much nicer it felt (though some of them missed the *Readers' Digests*!). The receptionist was absolutely delighted, claiming that everyone seems friendlier. All of them feel happier with a pleasant working environment – most of the partners have now decorated their own offices.

It is important not to fall into the trap of patronising people by thanking them when no thanks are really due. Human beings are very efficient hypocrisy-detectors, they can usually tell if someone's 'thank yous' are sincere or if they are delivered simply for some other reason (out of a sense of duty or to provide an incentive). Whilst the former create feelings of warmth and friendship, the latter can generate feelings of cynicism and distance.

REWARDING EFFORT AND ACHIEVEMENT

Rewards can take many different forms including:

- praise and thanks
- share-options, bonuses or increases in salary
- fun: parties/lunches/dinners/outings
- increased freedom of choice
- increases in status and/or power
- privileges and responsibilities.

All these things can be intrinsically rewarding to people, but all are additionally rewarding in virtue of their effect on self-respect. To be rewarded for having done something well is to be encouraged to feel pride in one's abilities.

> A comprehensive school in Northumberland allows pupils an hour's lie-in as a reward for exemplary attendance over a school year.

The choice of appropriate reward is important: managers in particular need to be aware that the sort of thing *they* would find rewarding would not necessarily be viewed as such by employees, suppliers, customers *etc*. It is also important to consider the prospective reward from every angle to ensure that there is no hidden sting in its tail.

> BT were taken aback by the lack of response to a promotion – a prize draw for a holiday with everyone on their Family and Friends list. Customers simply did not want to go on holiday with their bank managers, accountants, computer servers, lawyers and others who were on the list to attract the Family and Friends discount!

It is not only individuals who can be rewarded, of course, it is also teams, departments and indeed organisations as a whole.

Rewards can act as incentives. When they do it is important that they be:

- linked to efforts and achievements that are easily measurable
- chosen in consultation with those they are supposed to motivate (so they really will motivate)
- well-advertised so they can do their work as motivators
- awarded very soon after the effort or achievement for which they are providing an incentive.

As we saw in Chapter 5 the more people are involved in setting their own targets, choosing the incentives that will motivate them and evaluating their own performance against these targets, the more likely it is that they will achieve these targets.

> Six thousand Asda staff recently made a paper profit of £600 when their share option scheme matured.

If reward is tied too closely to results, however, this can *lower* performance. After all why should anyone set targets high when by setting lower targets they can be more sure of reward? When rewards are linked to particular objectives it is important that the package be negotiated and agreed in the light of organisational objectives.

> Ikea, the furniture retailer, handed over to its 40,000 employees its entire takings for Saturday 9 October 1999 as a 'millennium thank you'.

Organisations need to encourage people to set targets that are high enough to provide a real challenge, yet low enough to make achieving them a real possibility. When pitched properly the challenge of achieving a target is itself a motivator because of its link with self-respect.

> Richer Sounds, a Hi-Fi chain, owns a string of holiday homes which staff are allowed to use free of charge. It also gives each store or department £5 per head to have a few drinks in the pub to 'think about ways to improve the company'. Every quarter the best suggestion wins a prize such as day Grand Prix racing or hot air ballooning.

Rewards should not always act as incentives. Sometimes they should be awarded for their own sake as a return for good service or for extraordinary effort or achievement.

In Prêt à Manger's sandwich shops outstanding service can be rewarded at any moment. Mystery shoppers, served well, hand the team member who served them a gold card – the signal for hoots and whoops from other members of the team and the immediate payout, to the team member, of £50 from the till. Every month each estate (group of 8/9 shops) chooses, on the basis of reports from its mystery shoppers, its star team. The whole team are then treated to dinner at a local restaurant. If a team wins this prize three months in a row the team will go off for the weekend to a European destination of their choice. Twice a year, to say 'thank you', Prêt holds parties for the whole company (and its suppliers). Taking over a large chunk of Battersea, every member of staff can dance to live bands, simply mingle or enjoy the dodgems at the funfair. Those who have worked at Prêt for five years or more are encouraged to bring families and treated to lunch in a separate marquee. Prêt does not only reward staff with fun. The organisation has a clear structure designed to reward good service and willingness to take responsibility. A team member who shows initiative will soon become a 'team member star'. If he or she continues to make a significant contribution it will not be long before they are invited to go on a team leader course. Pay at each level is increased to reflect the extra responsibility. Prêt started with one shop in 1986. It now has 96 shops and a turnover of £100 million.

It is important to reward effort as well as achievement because effort is usually linked to achievement. Care needs to be taken, however, to ensure that the reward of effort does not replace the reward of achievement. When people get rewards for trying hard (without succeeding) this can sever the important psychological link between effort and success. When we try to do something we should be trying to do it successfully.

South-West Trains run a further education programme for their train drivers and other staff. Employees can qualify in foreign languages, information technology, car maintenance, electronics and other subjects. Several subjects are available at GCSE and A-level. The Open Learning Centres are open 24 hours a day, 7 days a week. The organisation set up the centres because they recognised that workers on shifts have difficulty attending other courses. The courses – especially those in IT – have proved extremely popular.

SUMMARY

An organisation can only succeed in living up to its values if its people understand these values and are willing and able to make an effort to help the organisation live up to its values.

Such hard work and good will deserve both recognition and reward. Both recognition and reward make people feel valued and this makes them even more willing to exercise effort and good will.

An organisation that creates a climate in which recognition is pervasive and reward frequent will be greatly enhancing its chances of success.

9

Looking to the Future

We have now completed our discussion of how to write an effective mission statement. To summarise, we have discussed a six step process the taking of which will enable you to:

- write a mission statement that is understood and agreed with by everyone in your community
- ensure that the values expressed in that mission statement inform every aspect of organisational behaviour.

The six step process involves:

1. Identifying, with your community, the organisation's aims and values.
2. Reviewing current practice to identify:
   - present success in living up to these values
   - opportunities for further work.
3. Identifying concrete objectives.
4. Planning and implementing desirable changes.
5. Monitoring progress and evaluating success.
6. Recognising and rewarding effort and achievement.

Taking the six steps will take time and energy. It will also cost you money. But the benefits to be derived from the proper execution of the six steps will be amply repaid.

ROLLING THE PROCESS

The six step process is not a one-off process. Organisations are like living organisms: they are constantly changing. As your people change, as your situation changes, as the world around you changes, you will find it worthwhile re-visiting the six steps of the process.

Many organisations have cycles that provide them with the ideal opportunity to re-visit the process. Such cycles include:

- the development-plan cycle
- the length of time pupils are at a school
- the term of a director or governorship.

They can, however, be chosen on an arbitrary basis: every five or seven years, perhaps.

The cycle you choose will be a reflection of the nature and size of your organisation. You do not want to go through the cycle so often that people start to treat it as an academic exercise. Nor do you want to go through it so seldom that you must start anew on each occasion.

Ideally, when you start a new cycle:

- At least 40 per cent of the people who went through it last time will still be with you.
- Sufficient time has elapsed to allow these people to be keen to re-visit the process.

Unless, since the last cycle, morale has dropped significantly, your reputation has been sullied or some significant change has been experienced, you will not need to spend as much time, energy or money in repeating the process.

Many of the techniques that last time you had to introduce, by this time will be securely embedded in organisational practice. By the time you re-visit the process people will be used to being appraised, to reflecting on objectives, and to planning the achievement of these objectives. They will not need to be convinced of the benefits of the process because they will have seen them for themselves. Much of the training that last time had to be put in place will by now have become part of the normal training process. The skills and techniques underpinning the processes and systems needed will be second nature.

Bringing in outsiders

For this very reason it is worth considering bringing in outside consultants to manage the process when you re-visit it. People within the organisation can become so imbued with organisational culture that they fail to see the warning signs that herald potential difficulties.

Complacency of this kind can undermine the effective operation of the six-step process. Outsiders can work with insiders to ensure that you get the best of both worlds.

REMEMBERING THE BENEFITS

In involving everyone in as many of the steps of the six step process as possible, and in rolling the process according to a sensible cycle, you will be ensuring that everyone in the organisation is:

- striving for the same goals
- working in accordance with the same principles
- adhering to the same standards
- fostering organisational morale
- securing the organisation's reputation
- building the character of the organisation.

An organisation for which all these things are true is an organisation with a healthy ethos, a culture that will bring success.

Nothing more needs to be said than good luck!

Further Reading

GENERAL

How are We to Live (Ethics in an Age of Self-Interest), P. Singer (OPUS books from Oxford University Press). A discussion of how we can continue to make life worth living under the stresses and strains of modern life.

Understanding Organisations, C. Handy (Penguin Business Management books). Classic text, extremely useful discussion of the nature of organisations. By the same author:

The Empty Raincoat
The Hungry Spirit
Gods of Management
The Age of Unreason

Emotional Intelligence, D. Goleman (Bloomsbury Press). Seminal book on emotional intelligence and why it can matter more than IQ.

101 Great Mission Statements, T. Foster (Kogan Page, 120 Pentonville Road, London N1 9JN). Just what it says, plus useful discussions of the process of writing mission statements.

In Search of Excellence, T. Peters and R. Waterman (Harper Row). Identifies the conditions necessary for excellence, especially where these pertain to employees.

VALUES

The Teaching of Values, G. Haydon (Cassell Studies in pastoral care and PSE). A book about the teaching of values in schools. It covers all the sort of values controversies likely to arise in schools.

A Good Enough Service, B. New (The Institute of Public Policy Research (in Association with the King's Fund), 30–32 Southampton Street, London WC2E 7AR). A discussion of the values of the National Health Service. This book considers whether, given the ineliminability of conflicts between values, the NHS is trying too hard to be perfect.

ORGANISATIONAL VALUES

The Character of an Organisation, R. Goffee and G. Jones (HarperCollins Business). A useful discussion of organisational culture and its relation to values.

Straight from the CEO, W. Dauphinais and C. Price (eds) (Nicholas Brealey Publishers). Interviews with and papers written by CEOs of top company. Many discussions of the importance of organisational values.

The Horizontal Organisation, F. Ostroff (Oxford University Press). A useful discussion about non-traditional ways of organising organisations. The emphasis is on delivery to the customer rather than (simply) internal efficiency.

IDENTIFYING OBJECTIVES

Target Setting and Goal Achievement, R. Hale and P. Whitlam (Professional Paperbacks, Kogan Page). Very useful book outlining the techniques of objective setting.

PLANNING CHANGE

Effective Change, A. Leigh and M. Walters (The Institute of Personnel and Development). Helps to plan change, anticipate problems and apply solutions.

MONITORING PROGRESS AND EVALUATING SUCCESS

Understanding Benchmarking, J. MacDonald and S. Tanner (Hodder and Stoughton, Institute of Management Series). Enables you to understand benchmarking in one week.

Understanding Investors in People, M. Peart (Hodder and Stoughton, Institute of Management). Enables you to understand Investors in People in one week.

SKILLS AND TECHNIQUES

The 'Management Pocketbook' Series, 14, East Street, Arlesford, Hampshire SO24 9EE. A useful series of small, short books covering techniques such as appraisal, assertiveness, presentation, communication, empowerment, interviewing, negotiation.

Talk Works, British Telecommunications plc, 81, Newgate Street, London EC1A 7AI. An extremely useful book on communication techniques, problems of communication and how to solve them. The book is supported by freefone numbers on which you can listen to examples of good and bad conversations.

Managing People, H. Williams (Prentice Hall, Essence of Management Series). Extremely useful discussion of leading by empowering.

FUND-RAISING

A Guide to the Major Trusts (The Directory of Social Change, 24, Stephenson Way, London NW1 2DP). A useful list of the top 300 charitable trusts and their main areas of interest. This book has a useful section on how to make a successful application.

Practical Fundraising, D. Wragg (Judy Piatkus, 5 Windmill Street, London W1P 1HF). A simple guide to fundraising from the jumble sale to business sponsorship.

Preparing a Winning Business Plan, M. Record (How To Books, Customer Services Dept, Plymbridge Distributors Ltd, Estover Road, Plymouth PL6 7PZ). Your fundraising is more likely to succeed if you make use of a clear, concise and well-thought out business plan. This book will help.

Appendix
Examples of Value Statements

On the following pages you will find some examples of value statements, drawn from the following sources:

1. Vision and Values: Civil Service Reform – *A Report to the Meeting of Permanent Heads of Departments, Sunningdale, 30 September– 1 October 1999.* Published by the Cabinet Office.
2. The HUB Initiative (The Institute of Directors Values Initiative).
3 Statement of Values by the National Forum for Values in Education and the Community.

Vision and Values: Civil Service Reform

VISION AND VALUES: CIVIL SERVICE REFORM

The Civil Service – Making a Difference

Our aim is to help make the UK a better place for everyone to live in, and support its success in the world. We want to be the best at everything we do.

In support of successive administrations, we will:

- act with **integrity**, propriety, and political impartiality, and select on merit,
- put the **public's** interests first
- achieve **results** of high quality and good value
- show **leadership** and take personal responsibility
- value the **people** we work with and their diversity
- **innovate** and learn
- work in **partnership**
- be **professional** in all we do
- be open and **communicate** well.

BEHAVIOURS TO GIVE EXPRESSION TO THE VALUES

Act with integrity, propriety, and political impartiality, and select on merit

When we do this well, we. . .

- assist the current administration, whatever its political complexion
- respect the common standards and principles that bind us together as public servants
- comply with the law and uphold the administration of justice
- base our advice on objective analysis of the evidence
- use public money properly, effectively and efficiently
- use merit as the only measure for selection of applicants
- uphold the Civil Service Code.

When we do this badly, we. . .

- misuse our official position or information acquired through it

- are negligent in spending public money
- allow our personal views to cloud our judgement
- frustrate the effective implementation of decisions by the administration on policies and services
- betray the principles of public service.

Put the public's interests first

When we do this well, we...
- know who are our customers are and what their needs are
- put ourselves in our customers' shoes
- give customers the quality of service that we would expect ourselves
- are courteous and helpful, even when under pressure
- involve citizens in government, actively gathering their views as we develop policy and deliver services
- mediate when there are conflicting interests and find a way forward.

When we do this badly, we...
- don't respond to what the public want from us
- focus on policy and procedure and the 'way things have always been done', rather than reaching an outcome that both we and the public will regard as a success
- develop and deliver policy and services without listening to the public
- are rude, obstructive or unhelpful
- fail to publicise and live up to clear standards of service.

Achieve results of high quality and good value

When we do this well, we...
- define a successful outcome and plan how we might achieve it
- take decisive action
- aim to achieve the best possible results
- think creatively
- anticipate problems and show drive and determination to overcome obstacles
- review performance and make improvements where possible
- celebrate success.

When we do this badly, we...
- act before thinking things through

- lack focus and direction
- fail to deliver work on time or within budget
- rest on our laurels
- give up when the going gets tough
- don't encourage feedback or monitor performance.

Show leadership and take personal responsibility

When we do this well, we . . .
- lead by example
- understand and communicate the bigger picture and our role within it
- work within our teams to generate enthusiasm, commitment and respect
- show drive and determination
- are prepared to challenge and to be challenged
- take action to improve things
- manage our time and organise our work effectively
- manage risk and accept responsibility
- look to the future.

When we do this badly, we . . .
- focus on the short-term
- are blinkered and driven by our own priorities
- emphasise problems, rather than look for solutions
- look for others to blame
- don't practise what we preach.

Value the people we work with and their diversity

When we do this well, we . . .
- use people's talents and encourage them to develop their potential
- respect and support those around us
- involve others in our work
- give and encourage feedback
- listen to others' views and give credit where due
- trust others to do a good job
- encourage a healthy balance between work and home life
- understand and work with the different approaches different people may take
- actively promote equality of opportunity.

When we do this badly, we ...
- are unaware of, or insensitive to, the needs and feelings of others
- try to run the show ourselves
- demand, rather than earn, respect
- fail to make best use of people's talents and potential
- talk rather than listen
- view difference, change and challenge as a threat.

Innovate and learn

When we do this well, we ...
- see learning as part of life for everyone
- understand our own strengths and areas to develop
- develop our own skills throughout our careers
- are open to new ways of working and new ideas from whatever source
- look for and champion better ways of doing things
- take managed risks
- review performance, gather feedback, and learn lessons from mistakes and successes
- measure ourselves against the best
- share learning with others
- use information and communications technology to improve the way we work.

When we do this badly, we ...
- are closed to new possibilities and opportunities and shut down new ideas
- stay stuck in a rut and stick with what we know - 'We've always done it this way'
- don't recognise our own developmental needs
- don't value learning
- see training and development as something that is done to us
- move from task to task without review and so don't benefit from experience
- blame people for mistakes, rather than learning lessons.

Work in partnership

When we do this well, we ...
- understand how everybody contributes to the shared goal
- share objectives
- work co-operatively with others to achieve the best possible outcome

- build and support networks
- use influencing and persuading skills to achieve objectives
- mediate conflicts to get to a win-win situation
- gain knowledge and experience of the world around us
- share good practice and solutions.

When we do this badly, we ...
- ignore others' interests
- fail to win respect and to be heard
- feather our own nest at the expense of others
- compromise to the lowest common denominator
- listen to the loudest rather than the truest voice
- keep information to ourselves.

Be professional in all we do

When we do this well, we ...
- implement policy and take decisions to reflect Ministers' wishes
- get best value for money
- do the best possible job we can
- are honest, fair and impartial
- understand the wider impact of our decisions
- take time to think about our work and how we do it
- evaluate the effectiveness of our work
- measure ourselves against the best.

When we do this badly, we ...
- accept mediocre performance from ourselves and others
- base our decisions and advice on assumptions
- tell others what we think they want to hear
- ignore the bigger picture
- don't look to improve on the way we do things.

Be open and communicate well

When we do this well, we ...
- are aware of, and make best use of, e-government and IT
- give people promptly and helpfully the information they are entitled to
- help people to understand government policies
- explain things clearly in plain English
- listen, as well as talk
- are approachable and helpful

- show courtesy, sensitivity and tact
- persuade and influence others, rather than telling them
- think about our audience
- think about the best way to get our message across.

When we do this badly, we ...
- keep information to ourselves without good reason
- use ways of communicating that we are comfortable with, rather than the best way
- fail to grasp what others are trying to say
- are seen as rude, frosty, tactless, or aloof
- write or speak in more complicated language than is needed
- are economical with the truth.

© Crown copyright 1999.

Source: *Vision and Values*: Civil Service Reform – A Report to the meeting of Permanent Heads of Departments, Sunningdale, 30 September – 1 October 1999. Published by the Cabinet Office.

The HUB Initiative (The Institute of Directors' Values initiative)

Statement of the purposes and values of business
The HUB national forum agreed the following statement:

- In Britain today the purpose of business is to trade profitably and reward enterprise and effort. It does this best while taking into account:
- The interests of the wider community
  - The values of honesty, trust, respect, responsibility, fairness and innovation.

Statement of Values by the National Forum for Values in Education and the Community

An extract from the preamble to the statement

- The remit of the Forum was to decide whether there are any values that are commonly agreed upon across society, not whether there are any values that should be agreed upon across society. The only authority claimed for these values is the authority of consensus.

- These values are not exhaustive. They do not, for example, include religious beliefs, principles or teachings, though these are often the source of commonly held values. The statement neither implies nor entails that these are the only values that should be taught in schools. There is no suggestion that schools should confine themselves to these values.

- Agreement on the values outlined below is compatible with disagreement on their source. Many believe that God is the ultimate source of value, and that we are accountable to God for our actions; others that values have their source only in human nature, and that we are accountable only to our consciences. The statement of values is consistent with these and other views on the source of value.

- Agreement on these values is compatible with different interpretations and applications of them. It is for schools to decide, reflecting the range of views in the wider community, how these values should be interpreted and applied. For example, the principle 'we support the institution of marriage' may legitimately be interpreted as giving rise to positive promotion of marriage as an ideal, of the responsibilities of parenthood, and of the duty of children to respect their parents.

- The ordering of the values does not imply any priority or necessary preference. The ordering reflects the belief of many that values in the context of the self must precede the development of the

other values.
- These values are so fundamental that they may appear unexceptional.
- Their demanding nature is demonstrated both by our collective failure consistently to live up to them, and the moral challenge which acting on them in practice entails.

Schools and teachers can have confidence that there is general agreement in society upon these values. They can therefore expect the support and encouragement of society if they base their teaching and the school ethos on these values.

THE STATEMENT OF VALUES

The self
We value ourselves as unique human beings capable of spiritual, moral, intellectual and physical growth and development.
On the basis of these values, we should:
- develop an understanding of our own characters, strengths and weaknesses
- develop self-respect and self-discipline
- clarify the meaning and purpose in our lives and decide, on the basis of this, how we believe that our lives should be lived
- make responsible use of our talents, rights and opportunities
- strive, throughout life, for knowledge, wisdom and understanding
- take responsibility, within our capabilities, for our own lives.

Relationships
We value others for themselves, not only for what they have or what they can do for us. We value relationships as fundamental to the development and fulfilment of ourselves and others, and to the good of the community.
On the basis of these values, we should:
- respect others, including children
- care for others and exercise goodwill in our dealings with them
- show others they are valued
- earn loyalty, trust and confidence
- work cooperatively with others
- respect the privacy and property of others
- resolve disputes peacefully.

Society

We value truth, freedom, justice, human rights, the rule of law and collective effort for the common good. In particular, we value families as sources of love and support for all their members, and as the basis of a society in which people care for others.

On the basis of these values, we should:

- understand and carry out our responsibilities as citizens
- refuse to support values or actions that may be harmful to individuals or communities
- support families in raising children and caring for dependants
- support the institution of marriage
- recognise that the love and commitment required for a secure and happy childhood can also be found in families of different kinds
- help people to know about the law and legal processes
- respect the rule of law and encourage others to do so
- respect religious and cultural diversity
- promote opportunities for all
- support those who cannot, by themselves, sustain a dignified lifestyle
- promote participation in the democratic process by all sectors of the community
- contribute to, as well as benefit fairly from, economic and cultural resources
- make truth, integrity, honesty and goodwill priorities in public and private life.

The environment

We value the environment, both natural and shaped by humanity, as the basis of life and a source of wonder and inspiration.

On the basis of these values, we should:

- accept our responsibility to maintain a sustainable environment for future generations
- understand the place of human beings within nature
- understand our responsibilities for other species
- ensure that development can be justified
- preserve balance and diversity in nature wherever possible
- preserve areas of beauty and interest for future generations
- repair, wherever possible, habitats damaged by human development and other means.

Source:
Taken from the newly revised *National Curriculum Handbook*.

Index